Using NLP to Enhance Behaviour and Learning

Also available from Continuum

Supporting Children with ADHD 2nd Edition, Kate Spohrer

Teaching Assistant's Guide to Emotional and Behavioural Difficulties, Kate Spohrer

Teaching Assistant's Guide to ADHD, Kate Spohrer

Teaching NLP in the Classroom, Kate Spohrer

Using NLP to Enhance Behaviour and Learning:
A handbook for teachers

Terry Elston and Kate Spohrer

network
continuum

Continuum International Publishing Group

The Tower Building   80 Maiden Lane, Suite 704

11 York Road   New York, NY 10038

London, SE1 7NX

www.continuumbooks.com

© Terry Elston and Kate Spohrer 2009

British Library Cataloguing-in-Publication Data

A catalogue record for this book is available from the British Library.

ISBN: 9781855394438 (paperback)

Typeset by YHT Ltd, London

Printed and bound in Great Britain by the MPG Books Group

Contents

Acknowledgements   vii

Introduction   ix
How to use this book   ix

1 What is NLP?   1
So, what is NLP?   1
What makes a good communicator   2
NLP presupposition 1   3
NLP presupposition 2   5
NLP presupposition 3   5
NLP presupposition 4   6
NLP presupposition 5   7
NLP presupposition 6   8
NLP presupposition 7   8
NLP presupposition 8   11
NLP presupposition 9   12
Start your journal   14
Conclusion   15
Chapter 1 quiz   15

2 Sensory acuity   17
Sensory acuity (awareness)   17
Filters systems – how we make sense of the world   19
Rapport   26
Eye movements   33
Case study: changing a poor spelling strategy   36
Conclusion   39
Chapter 2 quiz   40

3 The language of life – representational systems   41
The language of life   41
Research on VAKOG   43
Favoured Representational Systems   46
Ideas for reflection   47

Categorization of words in Representational System   50
Translation between representational styles   53
Summary   55
Chapter 3 quiz   55

4 Anchoring, reframing, and metaphor   57
Three very useful NLP techniques explained – anchoring, reframing, and
metaphor   57
Anchoring in the classroom   57
Reframing with children and young people   68
Metaphors   74
Case study: the use of metaphor   80
Conclusion   84
Chapter 4 quiz   85

5 Meta and Milton Models of hypnotic language   87
History   87
Deletion, distortion and generalization   88
The Meta Model chart   100
Milton Model   101
NLP in schools – language of persuasion   114
Chapter 5 quiz

6 Setting goals   123
Finding the right goals for you   124
Setting goals with younger people   130
Chapter 6 quiz   133

Neuro-Linguistic Programming glossary   134

Chapter quiz answer sheets   138

References and further reading   146

Appendix   149

Acknowledgements

Thanks go to all friends and family who have been patient while this book has been crafted. Also many thanks to Deborah Fraser for kindly allowing the use of her work on metaphorical poems.

Introduction

The only person whose behaviour you really have any influence over is yourself. The power that can be gained by accepting this premise is unlimited! So, to experience yourself as unlimited in the classroom as you would wish to be has been our intention, for you, throughout the writing of this book.

That Neuro-Linguistic Programming (NLP) techniques work has already been proven and because you have heard of the success of NLP may be the reason why you are reading this book right now. What we can do to teach these techniques to you is to guide you through a series of experiences and mindsets that will give you and other teachers what they seek; that is, compliance from your pupils and freedom and satisfaction for you!

But before you progress further with this book, we should warn you that you are going to be asked to try these concepts on yourself. NLP is an interactive process, and as such, experience of it is as important as understanding the concepts. For NLP to work in your classroom it needs to be incorporated into and integrated into your everyday practice, rather like a fish is to water; then you will be able to get it into the children's goldfish bowl. That way, it starts to automatically have effect in your school environment.

How to use this book

Imagine riding a horse through a forest of tall trees. You are flanked, slightly to the rear by two other horses and riders, you cannot see their faces but you can see them out of the corner of you eye. You are going at some speed, it's a comfortable speed, but nonetheless invigorating and full of onward momentum. The horse is good, sound, looks out for dangers and moves with a gait that is in rhythm with your body. You feel as though you are floating most of the time. The trees are rushing past you, the sun steams in through the gaps, creating shafts of light, and your clothes are flying in the wind created by the motion of the horse. You feel very free and empowered by this extra energy you have at your disposal, and even though you are not sure where you are going, you are happy to go on nonetheless because somehow it all feels right. From time to time you come to an obstacle, a fallen tree to jump, another to duck under, a steep slope to climb down – at each of these points you swiftly, almost without thinking, consider the options, the horse allowing you to make decisions but unconsciously transmitting guidance on what is possible and what is not. Your deeper mind makes a choice and off you go, over the tree, under the branch, down the slope, all smoothly executed and taken in your stride.

Well you might have guessed the two other riders are the authors of this book, Terry and Kate. We are here, right behind you! The book is like the horse that takes you forward carefully, but with momentum and at a speed that is appropriate for you.

We have written this book with a view to taking you on a journey. It's an experience rather than a goldfish bowl of content; therefore along the way there will be various techniques – or obstacles – to try out so that you can ingrain NLP into your heart, mind and daily actions. If you can envisage taking this ride from the beginning to the end of this book, we believe you will obtain the fullest benefit.

Note of use of terms. Throughout this book the term 'deep mind' is used to refer to what you may think of as unconscious mind or subconscious mind.

Using the book as a workbook, you will see spaces for jotting down your thoughts, but you may prefer to keep a completely separate journal; the choice is yours. Either write in the spaces here, or in your own book, or on a PC; whichever suits you. You might even want to record your thoughts and notes on audio or video. You may even prefer to discuss various aspects with a colleague, or to follow up with a course specially designed for the education practitioner. However you do it, enjoy the ride! – read on, get involved, keep a journal and prepare for transformation . . .

1

What is NLP?

In this chapter we

- look at the basic presuppositions (convenient beliefs) of NLP
- suggest a number of activities you can try out in the classroom that will reinforce the learning
- encourage you to start a journal to help you develop as a practitioner of NLP in the classroom.

From the perspective of an educationalist, what we know of as accelerated learning in education seems to be out of the same stable as NLP. Many other concepts – learning styles, multiple intelligences and Brain Gym – also have a neurological aspect that links them with NLP. However, NLP is so much more than this.

Over several years working in behaviour advisory work, research and training, casual observation has indicated that the basis of good teaching is a good relationship with your students. Our professional quest is to find ways to enable teachers and teaching assistants to gain this skill quickly, and nothing we have found has come up with these skills with the speed and effectiveness of NLP.

So, what is NLP?

NLP stands for Neuro-Linguistic Programming. Our neurological system regulates how our bodies function. Our language or linguistics influence our communication with others, and how we are programmed influences the models we create to make sense of the world around us. NLP was founded in the 1970s by John Grinder and Richard Bandler, who were based in California. They studied the communication styles of very gifted communicators and modelled their behaviour.

They found amazing and interesting results. By modelling the way excellent communicators work, they discovered (which is now proven scientifically) that most of us can improve our capabilities as we seek to be the best we can at whatever we do. So who wouldn't want to?

In 1975 John and Richard wrote the seminal NLP text *The Structure of Magic: A Book about Language and Therapy Volume 1* (Bandler and Grinder 1975). *The Structure of Magic* is a complicated read which drips with linguistic gems. However, many people have read the book and there are lots of training courses out there to help a practitioner get to grips with NLP and 'feel it in your bones'. Bandler was the practical one who believed in lots of action, while Grinder emphasized the academic side of NLP, therefore they provided us with a vast web of communication that we can benefit from.

What makes a good communicator?

I remember a teacher who was a great inspiration to me both at school and after I had left school. He always started his lessons with some kind of meandering story and I used to wonder just what the point of the lesson was, but I realize now that he was actually using story, or, more accurately, metaphor, to embed learning. He was preparing our deep minds for learning and using subliminal messages to drive home scientific points. He probably didn't realize he was doing it: he was just a naturally gifted communicator!

So what was it about NLP that seemed to draw me in so that I had to learn more? I was very sceptical for a long time; in fact I had looked at NLP for about ten years before I began proper training. I usually take some convincing that something is good but this is how it turned out to be!

NLP is based on practical experiences that have worked for someone at some-time. It doesn't mean, or say, that all NLP techniques will work for everyone, in fact almost by definition NLP is about individualizing responses, and calibrating (watching and examining) on the behaviour of others.

NLP is very effective in enabling people to overcome fears, phobias, anxieties, traumas, learning difficulties and limitations. NLP enables learners to achieve more in the school situation and to learn more effectively.

I once was sent a boy of about 12 years of age who was said to be disruptive and not learning as well as he could. He was on a card system and badly needed to perform better. I met with him and used basic NLP techniques, communication skills and good rapport to get into his world. After a short time he really looked forward to meeting me and sharing his way of being, which actually was very advanced. We got his results back to where he was considered not a nuisance and learning well and to top it all I was able to clear a phobia of heights for him as the cherry on the cake!

So, as you can probably guess, as well as being a book for your self-development, through you it can be used with the pupils who want to and can get on in class, this is particularly useful for children with special educational needs, or behavioural difficulties, and for those children who are troubled and hard to reach. Fears and anxieties produce a lack of confidence, poor confidence leads to poor self-esteem, leading to poor learning. If you are confident to take risks with your learning, you can experience being stretched, and growing as a result.

So, how do we do this?

The cornerstone of any of this specialized work is to achieve a rapport as quickly as possible with whoever you are working with. Then (we will look at rapport techniques a little later), a pupil or colleague will be connected with you on a deep enough level for the rest of NLP to start working its magic!

In the background we have a few operational beliefs that assist the whole process too.

NLP calls these presuppositions, yet you can think of them as convenient beliefs.

When you begin to adopt these presuppositions, your communication effectiveness will soar!

NLP presupposition 1 – 'A map is not the territory' and 'the menu is not the meal'

Our senses take in raw data from our environment but this raw data has no meaning whatsoever other than the meaning we choose to give it. This is an idea derived from Alford Korzybski who developed general semantics theory. His wording was 'the map is not the territory', but I feel for children the use of menus and food is more familiar and relevant. The menu should not be confused with the meal it represents. We don't actually eat the menu, it is simply a representation of the meal and very useful as a guide to what were are about to eat, but it is not the real thing: it differs in many ways – it's on paper or a board for a start, it is flat and not generally edible. Of course this is just a metaphor, and the real meaning is that each one of us has our own interpretation of the reality 'out there', i.e. the environment we find ourselves in – we understand reality according to our map or menu. We need this 'map' and could not function without it, but we also need to remember that maps and menus need to change over time; they need to be redrafted when we discover a new bit of 'reality' or our palate changes and we need a new menu.

Activity for the classroom

Enabling children to understand different perspectives is sometimes very easy. In fact adults can be more stubborn than the flexible mind of a pupil.

The idea behind the map is not the territory, or the menu is not the meal, is that everyone's reality is different and there is no one reality at all! Take an object that is fairly simple to draw but has something to distinguish its different sides. A box with a bold design on it might do, it could be a cereal packet. Place the object on a table in the centre of the room and arrange the tables and chairs around in a large circle. All the children will have a slightly different viewpoint, but they all know they are drawing the same object. You could give them colours to use (oil pastels are my favourite). See what they come up with. You can then discuss the different pictures from different perspectives and explore ideas; one being that although we may be looking at the same thing, we sense it in very different ways, therefore making our own reality. The philosopher and mathematician Plato remarked that the 'world of our senses are illusion!'

You may not get as far as this philosophy with younger children, but you might be surprised at just how far you can get. You can always refer back to this distinction when you need to help pupils understand different perspectives.

What came out of the discussions you had with the class?

Do you think you will be able to draw on this class experience to enable your pupils to look at a situation from a third perspective?

How long will it be before you do that – a day, a week, a term?

Here are a few more operational beliefs.

NLP presupposition 2 – Your perceptions are your *projections*

Candice Pert (1999) in her book *Molecules of Emotion: Why You Feel the Way You Feel* describes her theory on perceptions from the perspective of a research scientist, and also how she was sidelined in her discoveries. In the fabulous film *What the Bleep – Down the Rabbit Hole* (2006), Candice tells the story of Columbus and how, as he was approaching the Americas, the indigenous population looked from the shore and saw no ships. They had never seen these forms before and could not conceive of them, so they just didn't see them. They did see large waves, but no ships. Whether this is believable or not, on some level or another, we all do this. We make stories to fit our patterning; our mind then creates our reality. Only by experiencing new things and widening our horizons can we believe more things are possible. NLP can help anyone do this. If we can bust limiting beliefs, we can go to places we have never been before. Focusing on something positive can fire up every cell in your body and assist great transformations. This can be used for health, learning, confidence; the list is as long as you want it to be.

If you think about your students, you probably want them to feel able to do anything you ask them to do. They, on the other hand, may have limiting beliefs that stop them experiencing their full ability and reaching their full potential.

There are a number of further presuppositions.

NLP presupposition 3 – If one person can do something, anyone else can learn to do it

There is growing research and evidence to support the case that if one person can do something, anyone can do it! Skills can be infused and learnt. In fact this is how babies make progress, by copying other human beings, either successful ones or not!

Is there a skill that you would like your class to be really good at, or are there skills within the class that you would like to be shared around more evenly? If so, why not try getting your children to model excellence? When conducting my NLP Master Practitioner Training courses, sometimes I start a modelling section by blowing out perceived limitations of competence to start with. I'll ask if someone in the room thinks they are a poor catcher of a ball or any such objects. When someone steps up, I'll test them and notice how they are not good at catching. Then, I ask them to not worry about catching the ball at all, yet just watch which way the ball is spinning. I tell them they can even drop the ball and it doesn't matter. Then, guess what?! Of course, nine times out of ten they catch the ball easily, even though I may throw it even harder than usual.

This cute trick gets the class interested in how learning can be easier than they expect to begin with.

So, find something the class can model, such as juggling. Get a professional juggler to come in and allow the pupils to ask questions to find out how the juggler does it. Perhaps even what beliefs the juggler has, what's in their mind when juggling, or how they learned to juggle. This will achieve two things: one, they will learn a new skill, yet most importantly, *they will have learned how to learn.*

Jot down ideas you have about what your class could model.

NLP presupposition 4 – There is no such thing as failure, only feedback

I used to think that life was unfair and unjust. All life was filtered through this veil and even if things were going well, I used to perceive that sooner or later the trapdoor was going to open to failure yet again.

When I found out about NLP, I realized the presupposition *there is no such thing as failure, only feedback*, and my life changed. I'm not sure what happened, but we did an exercise where we stood on paper images of these sayings and I saw life differently. I had an oversight of my life and then saw that life is not about always having to 'win' – life is about a process of experiences and experiments, all leading to more learning and more experiences. When life is seen as a learning experience and not just about getting things 'right', your pupils can relax more into the feeling of getting feedback to encourage more excellence in what they do. When the emphasis is just on learning, the pupils tend to drop more balls!

Activity for the classroom

Alter the language in the classroom – drop the use of 'failure', 'see me', 'not good enough'. Firstly, the deeper mind does not like being challenged too strongly. If you praise something about behaviour first, then layer in what can be improved, you'll keep the baby, the bathwater and the bath itself! So, some of this will be challenging you as a teaching provider to change some of your own language. Are you up for that? Changing habits is like changing your wardrobe. Sounds like a good idea but it can take a while to get started. What I'd suggest is that you practise every second you have on appreciating (overtly as well as covertly) what you see in front of you, finding a positive element in everything and then giving feedback to it ... personally and at school. This applies to yourself as well! Give yourself a valuable compliment before layering in some possible changes.

> Praise log – Keep a log of new ways you have found to appreciate what's around you this week.

NLP presupposition 5 – Things are what we *think* they are

Alford Korzybski illustrated this in a lecture by going to his bag and explaining he needed a biscuit. He offered some biscuits around and some of the students took biscuits. He then revealed the packaging more fully – dog biscuits! The reaction from some of the students when they believed they had eaten dog biscuits was to feel sick. He said this proved people do not only eat food, they eat words too. So, you can see that the meaning that we as individuals attribute to situations is immensely powerful. We can use that to our advantage, or disadvantage, the choice is ours.

Activity for the classroom

Tell the above story and use it to start a philosophical discussion of the idea it puts forward. Ask the class what they would think if, for example, someone told them that the person next to them had six toes instead of five on each foot! Why, and in what ways, would they have to change their minds about something that didn't matter a few moments ago? Remember that, when you facilitate such a discussion, it is very important to stand back and listen. Children will learn and discover more if they come up with thoughts themselves; so, if you can promote discussion and help discussion to continue by questions or remarks such as use of the phrase 'yes, go on' when someone is stalling, this will allow them space and encourage them to keep going and dig deeper. Often as teachers we want to rush discoveries. People learn best in their own time.

How did holding back and asking questions like 'yes go on?' feel?

NLP presupposition 6 – Resistance is a sign of lack of rapport

We will move heaven and earth for those we love or want to impress. In situations where you have rapport, you can have a great deal of influence. Sometimes in our work we need to act as if we really love the young people we work with, even when we feel we don't. During my training, my mother, a retired headteacher, used to say to me, 'you have to love your children'. She is right! If you want to get the best out of them you have to really value and cherish them. If you take time to develop rapport, to get into, understand, the way they are thinking, you will find communicating with them and leading them through learning so much easier. If they resist you, go back and look at your rapport skills (which we will cover later on). Think about what you need to do to put them at their ease, to level with them. Make them feel you accept them for what and who they are, that you are meeting them where *they* are, not where you *want* them to be. Abraham Lincoln once said, 'to defeat an enemy, make them your friend'.

NLP presupposition 7 – We create our own experience

We are responsible for what happens to us. Once we can accept that we have the resources we need, it is only one small step to move into making things happen that we want to happen. If we don't make something happen that we have decided we want and we still really want it, we need to go back, look at what we are doing, and do it differently. If it isn't working, change the way we do it. Look at the way successful people operate in this field, what are they doing that you aren't? Is there something you could learn from someone else? When you have totally accepted responsibility in all areas of your teaching practice, there is only success or the road to success. If you don't, all you have is your reactions to life's events. Responsibility simply means 'ability to respond' rather than to react.

Activity for the classroom

With your class, identify a person to model who they consider to be successful. You can do this individually, or if you like as a whole class; you may like to tie it in with one of the popular shows such as *X Factor*, or *Strictly Come Dancing* – anything that shows success comes with perseverance and a belief in oneself. Look at the characters and deconstruct what makes them successful. At a future time, refer the class back to these people and how they 'do' success – encourage your class to model the positive aspects of the person's behaviour. What does the class think the person chosen thinks in the morning, in the evening? What do they have to practise every day? What pictures do they make in their minds of the success they achieve?

What did your class decide people 'do' to be successful? How will they adopt some of these excellent practices?

NLP presupposition 8

The person with the greatest number of choices and most flexibility in a situation is likely to get the best result. Flexibility of thought and behaviour leads to a greater range of choices. To get different results, you need to keep doing different things. Remember, 'if you always do what you have always done, you'll always get what you've always got'. Think about which type of person normally controls a situation or group? It's normally the kids!

So, why is that? Well, if you think about this more closely, you will realize that they will demonstrate greater flexibility in their actions/behaviours. They can simply perform to more extreme ends in the spectrum of communication (and I mean non-verbal as well as verbal).

The best stand up comedians are usually also the most flexible. They might get hassled, heckled and harangued, yet their responses and reactions enable them to combat whatever is thrown at them.

If you want to become an excellent communicator, you'll need to discover how flexible you can be in any situation. I received valuable training through being a member of a comedy group; the experience of comedy improvisation led to self-development which has enabled me to be fluid and flexible in my reactions to various situations. You may not have the time or inclination to do this, yet you can always train yourself to adopt different and effective responses in any conversations or communications you are likely to encounter.

Exercise

Try to develop an awareness and the confidence so that where there are situations in which you have opportunity to respond to events or to what is being said, you have at least two ways of acting/communicating. Use different situations to practise how flexible you can be. You might simply change your tone of voice. Or you might try to use different opening words or phrases than you tend to use at present. As you become more comfortable with these new approaches, you will find that you can change your reactions quite dramatically and to great effect. Practise doing a few things differently every day: it may be something quite major, like buying goods at a shop you don't usually go to, or it could be simply getting out of bed a different side (the right side we hope!).

Flexible communication log – Note down all of the times you were aware that you had fluid reactions and a choice of responses to situations. Also the number of times you did something differently, even thinking patterns!

NLP presupposition 9 – The meaning of your communication is the response that you get

It does not matter what you meant, what really matters is the reactions of others to your words, tone and actions. People respond to what they think you mean, which may be an accurate or inaccurate interpretation of your intended meaning. In the classroom understanding this is absolutely critical. To be able to communicate what we mean, we need to have an idea of how the other person communicates, we need to have tuned into them sufficiently and watched their response. How frequently have you found what you said has been completely misinterpreted? Stand back, look, listen, feel, get a sense of the other person and try to get into their skin – then you will start to understand what they are understanding or misunderstanding about you and what you said.

Again, it does not matter what you meant, what matters is what the other party feels from what you said. How many times have you said to someone 'I didn't mean it like that!' The important issue is what is the reality from the other person's standpoint, what exactly did they experience. It comes back to the difference between the map and the territory. We have to accept that other people might not construe something the way we do, so to be a successful communicator we need to listen carefully, listen to what they are saying, listen to how they are saying it, tune in, get rapport going, get into their skin, and to communicate in a flexible way so as to get our intended message across. That way we have a greater chance of achieving our aims and objectives in a given situation.

The only person you really have any control over changing is you. So, if your message is not getting across or is not having the effect you hoped it would, you need to change the way you are communicating. If you are seeking to relate to someone but they are not getting the message because of the way you are giving it, unless you change the way you respond to that person you will eventually find yourself being misunderstood, whereas you had thought you were doing just fine! View things in this way, i.e. the meaning of the communication is the response you get, and you will become less frustrated because you will have the ability to change things and not be a passive observer or victim of another's map of the territory.

People have all the resources they need to deal with whatever problems people have. Those of you who have done any counselling will be familiar with the concept of facilitating the client to find their own solution to their problem. This pre-supposition is really a rewording of that concept. Essentially, the biggest hurdle in problem solving is acknowledging you have a problem in the first place. Once you have done this, you can go on to find ways to solve it, reframe it, reinterpret it, or get used to it and start to enjoy it. Whatever, it changes from being the problem it was.

All the resources we need are inherent in our own physiology and neurology. Even if you cannot totally believe that at this moment, it's such an empowering idea to hold on to. Think about children and adults you know who keep making excuses as to why they can't do something. Often they will try to make you believe that circumstances beyond their control are stopping them from doing things, and often these excuses are backed by very convincing 'stories' indeed! In fact, might you even do a little bit of this yourself? Think though, for a minute, how it would feel to truly believe that you can affect your own success. One of the great things about NLP is that is opens up your mind to new possibilities. You cast away limiting beliefs that have been holding you back for years and years and become open to success. Each one of us has what we need to succeed.

Try this:

When next a child tries to convince themselves (and you) that they cannot do something, ask them 'what would happen if you did it?' Wait for the answer (or for them to consider), then say, 'What would happen if you didn't do it?' (pause again), and then, 'What wouldn't happen if you didn't do it?' This last question is a bit of a teaser and it doesn't matter what the pupil says – as long as they've properly considered the question.

These questions come from Descartes and he used them to test theorems in mathematics. They have now (well for over 500 years now!) been redesigned to filter out any untruths in a prediction. The truth will 'out' from asking the questions. These questions have the effect of filtering out untruths, of which any limitation that's self-imposed will be. Perhaps trial these questions with a friend or colleague first.

> Using Descartes questions, how did you find the child's thinking developed? Did you have the confidence to use these questions?

NLP presupposition 10 – Every behaviour is appropriate in some context

Consider this: no behaviour is wrong in itself, it is perhaps just not the most appropriate behaviour for the context. You can think of it this way: as we go about our business as human beings we are trying to make sense of the world and do the best we can. Essentially everyone wants to be happy; we all seek pleasure, sometimes though this struggle, the way we get that pleasure, will conflict with the wishes of someone else and may cause significant harm. Nonetheless, to the doer, it makes some kind of sense. It is worth appreciating this when working with challenging behaviour. Some behaviours really seem destructive and contrary to what a person says that they really want. If you, as the teacher, can suspend your initial reaction and look for an intention behind the behaviour, known as the 'greater intention' (see chunking up in the *Try this* section below), you'll be empowered, whereas you weren't before! We are not saying we condone the behaviour, we are simply rising above the situation where we ourselves are reacting and not responding. Here's an example: two children are fighting in the playground. Our initial reaction is anger and it's *wrong*. What if you were to stand back (not for too long of course), and look at what may be the intentions behind the behaviours. I once had a fight with a friend at school but all it was about was that a lack of respect that had occurred. I wanted the respect back, as well as my friend back. Looked at like this, a resolution would have been having my friend back, rather than a detention and waiting 30 years to have contact again!

Of course, if the subject does not want to take that journey with you, there's not much you can do, but you have done your part, so take satisfaction in that.

Try this:
Instead of moving straight into your normal mode of reacting the next time you are faced with a challenging child in the classroom, stop, turn on your peripheral vision and 'tune in' to the environment in front of you.

Then 'chunk up' to the highest possible intention that you could see from that pupil for doing the behaviour (for instance, playing up can obviously be about needing attention, needing attention is a call for love, etc.).

To 'chunk up', use the following sentence and train yourself to use it. 'What's the intention of. . .', or 'for what purpose this. . .?' You can actually ask someone this and if the question has been asked with respect and with an intention to find a higher meaning, the subject is more likely to respond by giving you the higher intention, there and then!

When you have the information you need to move forward with that child, start to talk from the place of highest intention – you will likely notice that they respond in a completely different way!

Start your journal

Now you have learnt a little bit more about NLP, it could be a good time to start your journal. You may already have been filling in the 'white spaces in the book', or you may not. Now might be a good time to go to your own private journal and jot down some inner thoughts and feelings about what you have been experiencing on your ride through the communication forests. To be a good teacher, teaching assistant, parent, etc., it is helpful to know yourself well. You may need to be candid with yourself and sometimes change the way you think about and do things. This is what I call reflective practice, and one of the best ways to be reflective is to keep some kind of log of your day to day professional and private thoughts and actions. If you can manage to use the journal at the end of the day, use it that way, or if you find it easier to make a log at the beginning of the day, then do that.

You may already have a diary and that is a start – it gives an idea of what is going on in your life, but it can be so much more than that and so much more useful to you. This book is about getting your best practices into the classroom, so in this journal think about addressing these questions first:

- How do I feel about my work in the classroom right now?
- Are there any areas or aspects of what goes on in my classroom that I would like to change?
- How do I know that I would like to change them?
- What have I done so far to address that change?
- How did I do that?
- Do I know any other teachers/TAs who do things differently, in a way I might like to emulate?

Once you have decided how you want to be, and looked and examined how other people achieve great results, you'll have some insights into what you want to work on. It's possible to 'model' the way great performers do things so as to come closer to the results you want. Remember why you got into this: what were/are your dreams; do you still believe in them, or have you forgotten them now, in the face of adversity? Part of being excellent in yourself is believing you can have life the way you want it. So much conditioning goes into having you believe that you can't have things the way you'd wish them to be! Look at all the reasons you contemplate regarding why you cannot have things the way you want. Be honest with yourself at this point; and then recommit yourself once more to the goals and aspirations that got you this far!

I once was homeless (albeit very briefly until I was offered a friend's caravan in his parents front garden to live in) and now I am a consultant to the Cabinet Office in Whitehall for NLP. Nobody can tell me that people don't have the resources to get what they want!

Conclusion

Congratulations on reaching the end of Chapter 1! Throughout the chapter, hopefully you will have been dipping into the activities and trying them out with your class. Hopefully, too, you will have seen how, when you really embrace the presuppositions of NLP, you can look at behaviours in a different way and, in time, effect positive changes in your classroom.

Have a go at the quiz below to reinforce your learning and then go to the back of the book to see our reflections on the questions.

Chapter 1 quiz

	True	False	Maybe
1. If you can control your mind, you can have the greatest influence over your own behaviour			
2. NLP is a theory-based discipline			
3. Modelling the way excellent communicators work can improve your communication skills			
4. Noticing a person's preferred communication style (visual, tactile, auditory, self-talk) can assist you in gaining rapport			
5. A good relationship with each learning style in the classroom has no effect on learning			
6. NLP can help people overcome fears, anxieties and limitations			
7. NLP has no place in the classroom, just in a theory class			
8. Rapport is the cornerstone of NLP			
9. Our reality is what we perceive it to be through our senses			
10. Presuppositions are simply convenient beliefs which are designed to see life through different glasses			
11. There is no link between your mind and your well being			
12. There is no such thing as feedback, only failure			
13. There are no resistant pupils, only inflexible teachers			
14. Flexibility achieves control			

15. The real meaning of your communication is the response that you get from others			
16. In NLP we believe that people don't have enough resources to succeed so we need to supply them for others			
17. No behaviour is wrong in itself, but it is not always the most appropriate behaviour for the context			
18. NLP requires you to change your own behaviour before you can expect a change from anyone else			

Answers and discussion can be found on page 138.

2   Sensory acuity

In this chapter we introduce you to:

- how NLP utilizes sensory acuity
- what filters are
- how to build excellent rapport quickly
- what eye movements mean.

Sensory acuity (awareness)

We all have an unconscious awareness of another person's responses. Think how much better you could be, or at least how much more consciousness awareness you could have, with a little fine tuning and practice. If we train ourselves to perceive another person's unconscious feedback by observing closely through our visual, auditory and kinaesthetic senses, we begin to notice responses that tell us lots of new things. Much of the time we go around believing that certain body postures mean certain things in general. The essence of NLP is to look at each person as an individual, and to calibrate (make well judged assessments of) their behaviour and not to impose your preconceived mind reading of the situation. Knowing what your pupils' responses will be to certain situations or requests you make of them can help you tremendously in tailoring requests to suit their communication style, which will help you to help them to succeed in school. You get a more peaceful classroom, behaviour improves, they achieve better results – everybody benefits! Enhancing your sensory awareness helps you to assess quickly when you are on or off track and to be able to realign or adjust to a different course quickly.

Here are a couple of exercises to try out.

Train up your senses!

You will need another person to help you with this activity, but again you could try it out with your pupils.

Ask the other person to think of something they like a lot. To make this work they really have to 'be there'; that is, get them into the same state they are in when doing the thing they love, then you will know what it looks like, be able to recognize, when the person is in a good state. You may think this is obvious, yet it's the finer distinctions that allow people like Derren Brown, the famous mind control expert, to be so masterful. If the subject, the person, is really not responding or has great difficulty accessing any kinds of states, you can suggest they look at, or explain, what they saw, smell what they smelled, feel what they felt, involve all of the senses if you can.

While they are recalling this lovely thing, notice the expressions: skin colour, skin tone, lip size, pupil dilation, breathing and anything else that gives you consistent feedback.

Use the table below to help keep track of observations.

	Like	Dislike
Eye pupil dilation, wrinkles around the eyes, eyes more closed than open		
Lip size		
Head position		
Breathing rate		
Breathing position, i.e. from top, middle or lower part of lungs		
Skin colour		
Skin tone		
Facial expressions		

Get them to 'clear the screen' (empty their mind), so they can now do something different:

- Now in the same way as in the above question, ask them to think of something they dislike intensely.
- Make the same observations, using the grid above to note the changes.
- Get them to 'clear the screen' once again.
- Now ask the person to choose any like or dislike at random and to really hold on to that, in their mind inside strongly.

Your job is to assess which state it is, the good one or the not good one. Get three correctly in a row and you can say you've cracked the code!

You can heighten your awareness in all sensory areas. Here is an auditory way to do this too.

Auditory sensitivity exercise

You will need two people to practise this exercise. Choose an A and a B.

A closes their eyes. B stands behind so A cannot see them in any way. Then A says a short sentence like 'Hi, my name is Terry.' Then B has to repeat this as accurately as possible (well perhaps change the name to their own). A then gives feedback to how close B is to getting this exactly correct. If it is close enough, A will get a definite feeling inside as it's so close to themselves. Do not be polite and say 'oh that's near enough' if you don't get that feeling. Coach each other in how to get to that feeling. Get it to that place, then change around.

By improving your skill levels you will be able to tune into the tone of a person's voice, even when they are trying hard to hide their feelings, and you will be able to tell whether or not they are happy about a situation or something you are asking them to do. You can, no doubt, recognize how this has very useful implications in the classroom. Much of our work as educationalists is about motivating children to learn, often when they don't really feel in a mood to do so. How much better you will be at motivation when you can read their feelings about something more accurately, and build excellent rapport. Combining these two skills will be invaluable.

Filters systems – how we make sense of the world

Human beings are bombarded with sensory stimuli all of the time. We cannot possibly respond fully to every stimulus we receive, so to cope we filter out a lot of the information coming to us by deleting, distorting and generalizing the data. When we receive information (and you will be doing this right now), we try to compartmentalize it into a format we are comfortable with. Our brain will be looking for models that it is already familiar with so that it can parallel the information it is receiving. Once we have sent the information through the sieve in our brain, and have checked it against our existing values, beliefs, attitudes, memories and language systems, we construct an internal representation of the information received. Simultaneously a state is created which will be evident from our physiology, and we exhibit certain behaviours.

Knowledge of how a person filters data can help that person understand themselves, and if applied to others it can help significantly in your communication with them.

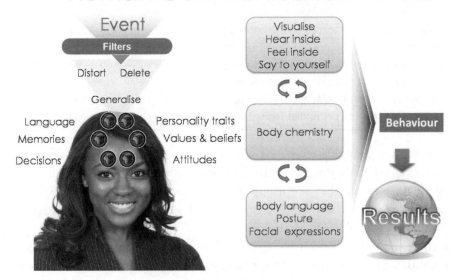

Figure 1

Generalizations

From quite early on in its life, the human infant is trying to make sense of the world around it. To do this the infant makes a lot of generalizations. This is a useful strategy: once you've learned how a door works, it's good to generalize this to other doors so we don't have to learn anew every time we are faced with the challenge of opening it!

However, this natural function can serve us negatively if we get lazy and start to generalize actions, clothing, and certain voice tones as meaning what we have learned from another being. We can often find ourselves making generalizations when we perceive something negative has happened to us. For example, we could feel all neighbours are nosey because our experience has been of one nosey neighbour. Having generalized beliefs like this (unchallenged by yourself) cuts us off from having more flexible and positive relationships with people around us.

Deletion

Because we receive so much information, we also employ a deletion strategy that helps us to filter out a lot of information because otherwise we'd go crazy! There's more information coming into your senses as you read this than you can possibly imagine. Research by Mihaly Csikszentmihalyi (1991) tells us that over 2,000,000 bits of information are coming into your systems every second! On the gross level of the senses, as I sit here writing this I can hear some quiet noises around me: as I make myself aware of them I realize I'm listening to a computer fan, and the fridge humming in the next room. Then there are all the microwave, infrared, high frequency sounds plus all the tiny pixels in every centimetre of space around me that I am not aware of but are all there nonetheless. However, I have been deleting these noises/pictures/feelings before my conscious mind even became aware of them. It means I can carry on with my focus on this work and not be distracted by extraneous information.

Of course some people and especially some children, particularly those with ADHD, may find this very hard to do and will keep being distracted by all this information. Other people actually need 'stuff' in the background to help them concentrate. To know how your class is dealing with all these details will increase the effectiveness of your use of such valuable information.

Distortion

Look at the following diagrams. Now perhaps you see how easy it is to get one meaning when there are others present.

Figure 2

We have to be careful we don't distort what other people's meanings are. It is easy to assume that because someone doesn't look at you and smile, they aren't bothered about you, whether they be a pupil or staff member. There may be many reasons for their behaviour, we simply don't know what they mean until we find out for sure. Complex people need more complex reactions!

Direction

The direction filter tells us what motivates a person into action. Some people move predominantly towards something they desire, while others move predominantly away from something they do not like. Most of us are some kind of mixture, but it's useful to know which one seems to be the bigger driver. This is particularly so in the school setting where motivation is a big factor in both getting work done and maintaining good behaviour standards.

Some people look for sameness in their preferences and others for differences. That's where the term 'stick and carrot' came from. In your class, some pupils will be looking for what is different, *not* the same. You could see these as 'mismatchers'. If you are looking for quiet, they will look for the noise (of course the noise would be different). If you want to have an orderly queue, they will see or act out *not* an orderly queue. If you are not on top of your game, these pupils can drive you to distraction!

'Differences' people can be very useful if given roles to play. For instance, if you and I were working on a complex project, it's good to have a difference person around to point out what we may have missed! With 'sameness' pupils, they will look for everything to be the same. They will see likeness in everything and one book will be like another and one story like other stories. They may miss some valuable data sometimes because of their tendency to generalize towards sameness!

Children who move 'away from' what they don't like may be less likely to respond to behaviour programmes with long-term goals and react better when given a reward up front that will be forfeited if they don't reach targets. Personally I would hate that, preferring to know that once I've earned it I keep it – but we aren't all the same! When you can work out what motivates people in this respect, you can alter your motivation directions accordingly. People who are very 'towards' need to hear what the possibilities are, what's great and what they'll be getting as a positive reward. 'Away froms' need more guidance about what is to be avoided, what *not* to be doing and how to keep away from pain, guidance always appealing to their desire to rid themselves of the thorn. For the most part you can use a bit of both, while watching out for the pupils who may be extreme in one or another.

When you know the way people respond to change in different situations you can use language which speaks more directly to them; for example, if they favour frequent change, focus on using language such as 'this is a completely different way to do this', or 'unique, special, never been seen before'. This kind of language will motivate them better than language that focuses on keeping things the same, such as 'we always do it this way, let's keep things the same as before, the way you did it before'. Do you see how this could help? Where people like to keep some things similar but change others, you need to use language that offers both, for example 'this is the same as before, but with a couple of great improvements'.

For 'away from' motivated kids, sometimes ask them 'not' to do something if you want them to do it (reverse psychology). You just have to watch out for the smart ones who will play with you whichever way you go!

> Select a couple of children you teach and see if you can identify whether they are predominantly towards or away from people. Then manage your language accordingly for each of them separately. How did you work it out?

Are you a 'towards' or an 'away from'?

Try the following to determine where you are on the scale of 'towards' or 'away from'.

How long do you stay in a job? Or even if you do stay in a job a number of years, how often do you want to change departments, or classrooms even?

If the answer is one year or less, you would come under the 'differences' type and will need a lot of change in your workplace. Knowing this, you can consciously make changes when you feel it's right. Even changing the classroom about a bit will suffice.

If you stay in your profession/classroom (and it feels alright) for three to five years you will be sameness with some differences. In other words, you'll be okay for that time and need some change after that. Longer than that, you would fit into the 'sameness' category.

Here's another way to find out easily a person's preferences.

Place three coins on a table, two of them facing upright with (let's say) the queen's head towards the top and both facing the same way. Have the third coin with the queen's head facing diagonally or horizontal to the others. Then ask the question, 'What's the relationship between these two coins?' The answer is either:

Same

Different

Different with sameness

Same with differences

The answers will give you some indication of your/their preference.

What can you learn from these observations? After becoming more aware of this filter, you will notice that some pupils look for similarities and the familiar and others seem to be looking more for difference. The latter may seem a bit oppositional because they can always come up with a counter-argument. Value this quality in young people, as it can be used to great effect. They may spot something you don't, and to them it could be a great discovery.

Action

The action filter determines how quickly a task is started, and I feel sure you will agree this is particularly relevant to the classroom. Differences in this area can cause real frustration. Some pupils will get on task straight away, whereas others will ponder and wait. As teachers we can become very frustrated by pupils not on task. We feel we have explained everything in sufficient detail to enable the young person to get on task, yet after the rest of the class have started, they still haven't begun. It may be that some students just need more time to get used to an idea, and there may be a lot of assessing going on in their mind which is not obvious. Some people like to think a lot before they act, whereas others act before they think. It is true that something between the two is probably the best way to be most of the time, but there are times when being very quick off the mark is useful, and times when taking time to study before you act is useful too. Get to know your own style and the style of pupils who you feel are harder to teach than normal. When working with pupils who are motivated to get on task straight away, then direct them towards doing so; however, with thinkers and ponderers a remark such as 'have a think about that for five minutes' might do the trick. This way you provide a time frame and keep things moving forward; they feel satisfied because they have had their bit of thinking time, and you as teacher still set the agenda.

Chunk size

The chunk size filter is particularly critical in the classroom and easily overlooked. If you deliver information in chunks that are the wrong size for the learner you could be missing a lot of learning opportunities. Some people like to have a lot of detail and information, whereas others will just want a quick sketch and only be interested in the 'big picture' concepts and become very bored with details – with these people less is more. Some people need details first, then the overview; others like the overview first to get them interested in the idea, then the details to give them the basis on which to work. If you can appreciate that all of these types and shades in between will be in your classroom, it will help you to tailor your information giving more appropriately. It could be also that some children will be better instructed in written form rather than by listening to you. To find out, listen to their conversation and if they use a lot of specific language you know that you need to match that style in delivering instructions. If they tend to be brief in their responses, that's probably the way they like to receive their instructions. If you remember that the conscious mind can only handle between five and nine pieces of information (from the book *The Magic Number 7*, by George Miller), this will help you to manage their learning chunks. Match this style and you will find communication easier and achievement increases.

External behaviour

This filter arranges people along the introvert/extrovert continuum. Although in school we try to get pupils to work well both alone and with others, it is worth bearing in mind that we don't all enjoy these two methods of working to the same degree. As adults we will often wish to go off alone to work when we need to concentrate on a task. For instance, right now I am sitting alone writing this, I could not do this work if I had another person close to me, that would distract me too much. This doesn't mean of course that I am an introverted person, but it does mean I work best on this type of task alone. Other tasks may be different; in contrast to the previous analogy, when I am in the garden I like to feel there is someone else out there too working with me.

Look out for how introverted and extroverted your pupils are in certain task-orientated situations. Calibrate their behaviour and set up situations that will maximize achievement.

Rapport

The three R's – Rapport Reduces Resistance

Here's how to keep building your rapport skills. Aim for a symbiotic relationship with your pupils – you need them as much as they need you!

Look at your own behaviour in those areas, be critical, give yourself some honest feedback, imagine looking on from a third person perspective, be self-aware. Only by being good at building rapport yourself can you pass on this very important skill to your class. You can do it!

How to build excellent rapport

A fantastic place to start in building a good relationship quickly is to attain good rapport with the other person. Basic NLP provides a toolbox of techniques, which offer ways of building good rapport effortlessly and unconsciously. Anyone can become a better communicator and start to build better rapport with those you wish to.

Imagine being able to have insight into what the other person is thinking at particular points during a conversation, and being able to respond to such insight and understanding with your conscious use of language patterns that you will be learning in this workbook. This may be the edge you have been seeking to enhance your powers of persuasion. Listening to the language people use gives you clues as to how your pupils are processing language. If you can mirror their style more accurately, you can enhance your communication with them. You can harmonize with them and draw out the learning more effectively. If this is something you would like to know more about, have a go at the exercises below.

Mirroring

Mirroring is physically placing your body in the mirror image of another opposite you (as if in a mirror). This needs to be done with respect and subtlety or it will look false and silly. Do not be afraid to try it however, it really does work, and to begin with you can practise with a friend who will not mind you playing with their movements to gain a greater connection. When you feel comfortable doing these actions and start to use this technique to gain connections, you'll realize how precious the technique is! People will feel acknowledged and will appreciate your interest in them. I rarely have to 'turn on' my rapport techniques because there is normally so much naturally occurring good feelings present in any situation to begin with. It certainly is useful when you need it though! One time my car got towed away from outside my house. It was kind of parked near to a small sign saying 'don't park outside number 23 on Saturday', but was so small and such a similar colour to other signs in the street that I missed it. I decided to dispute it, even though I knew the chances of me winning were very small indeed. When I got to court, I knew I needed to gain rapport quickly, so I dropped my pen on the floor to see which way the barrister's legs were crossed. Even though we can only see above the table, the deep mind is so smart, it knows if bodies are aligned or not! After a short chat, the barrister was looking with me for extenuating circumstances, so he could get me off, which he did!

Here are some examples of what there is to match and mirror:

- Body movements
- Size of information chunks
- Volume of voice
- Pitch of voice
- Tone of voice
- Topic interest – the words used
- Breathing rate.

Another example of making rapport work positively was when I was at Heathrow Airport and needed to only check in hand luggage as someone was waiting in Stockholm to pick me up. The airport assistant weighed my bag and informed me it was 4 kilograms too heavy! I looked at her and smiled, placing my attention on connecting with her and matching her energy and to a certain extent, her body language as well. I said, 'What can we do?' She said, 'Well it's too heavy.' I said, 'I know, what can we do?' She then told me I could put some clothes in my computer bag, but my carry-on bag was still 3 kilograms too heavy. Once more I said 'What can we do?' She looked around and then just waived me on! As soon as I was around the corner I could just put my clothes back in the bag anyhow. Good for rapport!

Matching

Matching can have a short time delay, but is very similar to mirroring in other respects. If someone is making a particular movement or gesture as part of explaining a point to you, you would of course be attentive to what they were saying but, then, when it is your turn to speak you could use a similar kind of gesture to explain your point. Unconsciously you will be recognized as someone who understands and 'speaks my language' and therefore listened to more intently.

The point of matching and mirroring is to eventually *lead* the situation, whatever that is. When you feel like the two (or more of you) have 'clicked', you can move into the leading phase, because there is sufficient trust and relatedness.

When matching and mirroring to a group, simply pick out the ring leaders or the most vociferous in the room and match and mirror them. Rapport leaders will change from time to time, so it's a good idea to be present to what's happening from moment to moment.

Practising these skills enables you to build up trust and your ability to lead children in learning will be enhanced.

Rapport activity

You can try doing a rapport exercise for yourself by following the instructions below. You will need two other people to help you practise this.

- Person A begins to tell person B about an experience at work or a personal experience. Person C watches A and B (i.e. observes them) and will comment later on what they were doing.

- C, you need to be watching for all of the things described below, so please read the notes carefully.

- B matches and mirrors (as described above) A by making the same kind of movements as A. You are in a conversation, so contribute to the conversation, and try to match their style of talking. If they use lots of visual language, you use visual language too; if they use auditory, you use auditory. Also, look out for the chunk sizes of the pieces of information they are offering to you. Match the size of information you give to the size they are giving you. This may feel strange to begin with and it is true you are in a false situation, but just go ahead and do it. It's not all about just being a monkey and copying; it's more about really being with the person opposite and showing their deeper mind that you are the same and there is no threat. Here's a great way to test rapport skills out: start by agreeing with the other person about something and DO NOT match and mirror. On purpose, MISMATCH the bodies (make this as extreme as possible so as to rigorously test the technique). Then find something you DISAGREE on and MATCH the bodies and energies. Use some of the criteria below to assist you.

- As you are doing all of this notice any feelings of comfort and discomfort you may have as they occur. What is happening when you feel good or not?

- Notice what is going on internally in your body as well as externally.

- Establish total rapport. You will know when you go into rapport. You will feel easier. Notice your FEELINGS as you go in to rapport.

- After about three minutes you should notice the physiological feelings of rapport.

- Also look for outward signs of rapport.

- Now move on to involve matching the voice – try to match tone, volume and intonation.

- Don't forget to match breathing as well.

- If a person has a bad behaviour or language you don't want to match, then match the energy of the person while using non-confrontational words. Most teachers either try to get louder or quieter than a pupil who is presenting a challenge. That's a 'mismatch' and will not serve much purpose.

> How did that feel? Discuss with each other (and C as well if there is one).

In a real-life situation the other person is not aware that you are *trying* to establish rapport. It just happens to them and they feel easier. So in real life, once you have become consciously aware of the skills yourself, it is much easier than doing it in a set-up situation like this. You can try this with anyone – on the bus, train, at work and even with the family if you want to experiment there!

Gaining rapport through matching the voice

You can practise different aspects of rapport skills, which when put together will blend synergistically and produce great results. One way is to concentrate on the rate of breathing and the vocal quality of the speaker. Have you ever noticed how if you listen to someone with a different regional accent to yours, you begin to find yourself slightly taking on some of the intonation of that person, and you may even pick up phrases and nuances of their speech. This is because you are falling into rapport with them. You have an unconscious desire to communicate more effectively with them, and so you make yourself more like them. It isn't mimicking or taking the mickey, it is flattery and a normal response to another human being you want to communicate with. Imagine then that you do not particularly warm to someone, but you know that for work purposes you need to get on well with them. That's when the technique of rapport comes into play.

Activity for the classroom

Focus on the child in the class who you find it hardest to get on with. Observe the timbre of their voice, is it high, or low, does it range a lot, or a little, does it grate on you, or is it mellifluous? What is the volume like, the speed of delivery?

It is very likely that however they talk it is in stark contrast to your preferred speech patterns, but you are there to communicate with your pupils, and one of the presuppositions of NLP is 'the meaning of communication is the response you get'. If you are not succeeding with a child, then your communication method needs to change, maybe a slight change in your timbre to match theirs might just be enough. Play around with this idea until you feel more resonance with the child's speech.

Work on establishing total rapport. Notice feelings of comfort and discomfort as they occur. Notice what is going on internally in your body, as well as externally. Notice FEELINGS as you go into rapport. After a few minutes you should notice the physiological feelings of rapport. Also look for outward signs of rapport, which would be flushing of the face, dilation of pupils (eyes that is!), and a feeling of connection, as if you've known them a long time.

> Describe how it felt to start to get rapport with someone you have previously found very difficult to get on with.

If you are not getting the results you desire, regard your communication as inflexible, rather than your pupil being resistant.

In our role as the adult amongst pupils, we want to keep finding ways to communicate effectively with them so that the response we get from our communication is the one we want to get. If we get a different one, we need to find another way. In Greek mythology Procrustes had an iron bed onto which he invited guests to lie down. If the guest proved too tall, he would cut their legs to fit; if the guest was too short, he was stretched out until he fitted. If we wish to behave like Procrustes, we would expect everyone else to fit our standard. However, it would be more sensible to try to adapt – to have a bed that is more accommodating!

As an exercise for yourself, take the child in the class who you find most difficult to communicate with. Work hard at building rapport, make an extra special effort to do this, and then see how as you build rapport you find yourself beginning to like the child more and they seem to like you more; you will also realize that you are becoming more flexible in the way you communicate. You may even find yourself saying, 'I would never have dreamed of saying that a few weeks ago', and you might find yourself starting to extend how you interact. Notice, too, how your class is starting to build better rapport with each other. Everyone benefits!

How did gaining rapport with this child make you feel?

Pacing – getting into step

In conversation with a friend of mine the other day, somehow we got to talk about walking in step. She remarked, 'Have you ever noticed how when we are walking along the street we always seem to be in step with each other, even though we have different sized legs? That's something I don't get with everyone, some people walk so quickly I just can't keep up, they rush me; then others are so slooooow, I get frustrated and impatient, and then I'm the one going off ahead.'

In fact, that walk is actually a metaphor for our relationship; this same principle can be applied to other situations, not just walking along the street with a good friend.

A young teacher in her second year of teaching one September described observations of her new class: 'They are so different from my last class, I know that they are a year younger, but it has really brought into sharp focus the relationship I had with my old class, the great rapport we had in the old class, but you know, I think I can speed up that rapport building by gauging the natural pace of the group, it's almost like finding a kind of "resonant frequency" for the group, and when I have hit on that I can harmonize with them and the result will be doubly good if I can resonate too.'

I loved this description; although it's all about sound waves, for me it created great visual appearances of waves doubling in size and energy being harnessed for everyone's benefit, a real gathering of momentum.

Activity for the classroom

When we work with groups of people our task is not just to get into rapport with individuals, but to get into rapport with the group as a whole, we need to sense where that group is; it will not be going at the same speed as the individuals because those speeds are all different, the group itself forms its own identity. With a little reflection you can sense that and work with it, not against it.

Over the week, keep a note of the mood of your class, with particular reference to pace; use the table below to help prompt your observations. You may also reflect on what you found and what you did intuitively to gain better rapport. You will know when you have rapport with your class because they will effortlessly follow your lead. Remember, this is simply observing what is going on in the room and what your response is. Later we can look at more appropriate responses that can lead your group more effectively.

Date:	Observation	Response
How fast/slow is the settling down time?		
Who is setting the pace?		
What is the general completion of work time?		
Did you achieve what you wanted to?		
Are you trying to put too little or too much into lessons?		
Where do you believe the ideal pace lies?		
Any other questions relating to pace		

Body and mind inextricably linked

Anything happening in the mind also happens in the body and vice versa. Deepak Chopra (1989) cites the neurotransmitter as being the communication device of the mind. These neurotransmitters are bathing every cell in your body. Therefore every cell is listening intently to every thought emitted from your mind!

This has particular implications for your body language. There is a saying in NLP that 'you cannot not communicate'. That's because your deeper mind will always be commenting on something and showing it through the body. Really, the body can't lie! We all give off unconscious signals that other people pick up on. Therefore it is useful to become aware of your own signals through your body (remember that another person will be more inclined to believe your body language than your words).

You can then start to be more aware of unconscious signals of others, and start to master the knowledge of the 'unseen' world of communication.

Eye movements

There is no doubt that one of the most fascinating and at the same time controversial aspects of what Richard Bandler and John Grinder modelled in the 1970s was eye accessing cues. In their work they had begun to notice that there appeared to be a correlation between where people's eyes look and the kind of sensory language they were using. More particularly, they suggested the eyes move around when people are thinking and internally processing (prior to speaking), and that you can often see a correlation between what they then say and where their eyes were before they spoke. Next time you're having a conversation with someone, pay particular attention to what happens to their eyes when they are thinking, particularly after you asked the question. Do you see any patterns or themes?

From their work, Bandler and Grinder discovered (as did Robert Dilts also) that as people recall certain parts of information, their eyes will move to certain quadrants of their brain to access either visual, auditory, kinaesthetic or self-talk. This then gives you a good idea about what that person is doing inside their mind as they try to recall information. They also observed patterns of relationship between the sensory-based language people use in general conversation and, for example, their eye movements (known as eye accessing cues).

A common (but not universal) style of processing in the West is shown in the chart (overleaf), where eye flickers in specific directions often seem to tie into specific kinds of internal (mental) processing. NLP also suggests that sometimes such processing is associated with sensory word use, so a person asked what they liked about the beach may flick their eyes briefly in some characteristic direction (visual memory access, often upwards), and then also use words that describe it in a visual sense ('The sea looked lovely', and so on). Likewise, asked about a problem, a person may look in a different direction for a while (kinaesthetic access, typically down-wards to their right) and then look puzzled and say 'I just can't seem to get a grip on things'. Taken together, NLP suggests such eye accessing cues are idiosyncratic and habitual for each person, and may form significant clues as to how a person is processing or representing a problem to themselves unconsciously.

Auditory cues

Figure 3

Remembering sounds (side left)   Constructing sounds (side right)

Visual cues

Figure 4

Constructing pictures (up right)   Remembering pictures (up left)

Making pictures (defocused)

Kinaesthetic cues

Figure 5

Accessing touch, taste, smell, feelings
(down right)   Hearing internal dialogue/chatter
(down left)

The most common arrangement for eye accessing cues in a right-handed person (these diagrams are to be seen as if you are actually looking at them).

It is important to remember NLP does not say it is 'always' this way, but rather that one should check whether reliable correlations seem to exist for an individual – we always need to calibrate on the individual level, but once you have learnt someone's pattern of operating you can start to make predictions. The common Western layout of eye accessing cues appears to be as shown below. Remember, this is as if you were looking at someone's face.

Visual construct (VC) – top left quadrant   Visual remembered (VR) – top right quadrant
Audio construct (AC) – middle left quad   Audio remembered (AR) – middle right quadrant
Tactile (K) – bottom left quadrant   Audio internal (or AD) – bottom right quadrant

Questions to ask someone to find out what's happening ... watch the eye patterns!

1. **Visual remembered:** Think of the colour of your car. What kind of pattern is on your bedspread? Think of the last time you saw someone running. Who were the first five people you saw this morning?

2. **Visual construction:** Imagine an outline of yourself as you might look from six feet above and see it turning into a city skyline. Can you imagine the top half of a toy dog on the bottom half of a green hippopotamus?

3. **Auditory remembered:** Can you think of one of your favourite songs? Think of the sound of clapping. How does your car's engine sound?

4. **Auditory constructed:** Imagine the sound of a train's whistle changing into the sound of pages turning. Can you hear the sound of a saxophone and the sound of your mother's voice at the same time?

5. **Auditory digital** (internal self-talk): Take a moment and listen to the sound of your own inner voice. How do you know it is your voice? In what types of situations do you talk to yourself the most? Think of the kinds of things that you say to yourself most often.

6. **Kinaesthetic remembered:** (Tactile) When was the last time you felt really wet? Imagine the feelings of snow in your hands. What does a pine cone feel like? When was the last time you touched a hot cooking utensil? (Visceral/Emotional) Can you think of a time you felt satisfied about something you had completed? Think of what it feels like to be exhausted. When was the last time you felt impatient?

7. **Kinaesthetic construction:** (Tactile) Imagine the feelings of stickiness turning into the feelings of sand shifting between your fingers. Imagine the feelings of dog's fur turning into the feelings of soft butter. (Visceral/Emotional) Imagine the feelings of frustration turning into the feeling of being really motivated to do something. Imagine the feeling of being bored turning into feeling silly about feeling bored.

Application in the classroom

In terms of learning and education, this knowledge of eye patterns can be really useful as you can begin to tell where your pupils (via their pupils) are trying to access information from and what strategies they are using to get their information. For instance, if you ask a person to spell a word, and they are looking down to the ground to their right-hand side they will be accessing feelings, so it will be no wonder that Charles would not be a very good speller. Try to spell a word by feeling it is probably the worst strategy you can imagine. Also, if the person looks to their left-hand side in the middle (see diagram), then they'll be trying to spell the word by hearing it phonologically: also, not the best strategy to use! You can't even spell 'phonologically', phonologically! Let's try . . . fonologically . . . nope!

You can improve people's spelling ability or learning ability by teaching them how to use the visual aspect of their brain. When you have developed the knowledge and skills so as to teach this to pupils, you'll see the remarkable effect it will have on them. Of course, this isn't just useful for pupils, this will also be useful to you in any conversational or negotiation situations where it's important for you to know how the other person is processing their world.

Case study: changing a poor spelling strategy

Pick somebody who spells particularly poorly but is motivated to spell differently and better. Ask them for a word that they cannot possibly spell. Catherine Sprackling, head of French at a Brighton school performed this technique shortly after being trained how to use it.

What Catherine did was to take a pupil and choose a word he could not possibly spell and believed he could never spell. Then she wrote that word on a piece of paper and chunked it into three parts. She used her knowledge of anchoring to make the boy feel good about the prospect of learning (you could just ask the pupil if there's been a time when they didn't think they could learn something and then they did). Catherine then showed the word, piece by piece (you can also make the chunks different colours to aid the visual aspects). She got him to recite each chunk of the word, while holding the word in his visual recall quadrant (VR). She would take the paper away each time but ask him to keep visualizing the chunk of word in his mind (watch their eye patterns to make sure they stay in visual recall). Then finally, she took away all of the chunks and asked him to spell the whole word, which he did successfully first time. Then to the amazement of the rest of the classroom, she got him to spell the word backwards with no more revision. He did it perfectly!

Other uses of eye patterns

The best-known therapeutic application of eye patterns has been undertaken by a woman called Francine Shapiro (1995), and is called EMDR which stands for *eye movement desensitization and reprocessing*. Her methods are now widely used in the process of therapy, and although not fully understood, they seem to work by linking the different areas of the brain together.

History

Dr Francine Shapiro, the creator of EMDR, is a licensed psychologist and a senior research fellow at the Mental Research Institute in Palo Alto. She is the Executive Director of the EMDR Institute, which trains clinicians in the EMDR method. She is the recipient of the 1994 Distinguished Scientific Achievement Award presented by the California Psychological Association.

So, how does this work?

Like a narrative, a piece of writing, a script is an instrument for the management and effective control of a play, film or broadcast. In this counselling/therapeutic context scripts are the tools with which we manage our adult life. You could call them language patterns (and in this case they can be pictures, sounds, feelings carried in language).

From our earliest and formative years we build a library of scripts through and with which we respond and react to life. As with the section on anchoring in Chapter 4, any stimulus is categorized and linked to our response and via our memory is stored in our database or library. What seems to happen is that certain areas of the brain or mind get underused or not even accessed for varying reasons.

For example, we will have a family of scenes about school which would include positive and negative affects depending on our relative success or failure regarding different aspects of our school experience. These scenes will be held in VR, VC, AR, AC, K and AD. If a scene is too painful, that area will be avoided.

A friend of mine was once asked a question by a teacher. My friend looked up and to his left (visual recall or VR). The teacher then shouted 'it's not up there boy!' That area may well be painful to visit the next time he's looking for information!

With the following exercise, you get a chance to link up all the different areas of the brain and literally exercise the different quadrants, linking them together so they all can work as efficiently as possible by using a grid reference from each quadrant to every quadrant on the eye map and moving a finger line all the way around (see diagram) accessing all the different areas.

Try this:

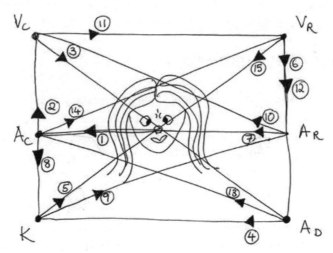

Figure 6 Eye tracking

1. Hold a pen out in front of you (about two feet in front your own or another's face).

2. Move it to the periphery (boundary) of the eyes to the left, so without moving the head, the eyes can just about still see the tip of the pen.

3. Move the pen and while superimposing the grid reference to your own face (or to another's face in front of you), follow the grid lines with the pen while keeping your head still and only moving your eyes.

4. Remember to go to the edge of the eyes' movements as you come to each end of a line.

5. Follow every possible line and join up all the lines by following the tip of the pen with the eyes.

6. If you find any glitches (places where the eyes flicker or do not move along smoothly), you can move the pen up and down that line until the glitch rubs itself out.

7. At the very least, this exercise will increase the coordination of each quadrant of the brain, causing more communication between areas that may have been less flexible before.

What this exercise does is to stretch the peripheries of vision, while connecting up every possible quadrant of the brain. This can help even the brightest of pupils, yet EMDR has had an amazing effect on all age ranges and in all sorts of different contexts.

Fourteen controlled studies support the efficacy of EMDR, making it the most thoroughly researched therapy method ever used in the treatment of trauma. The five most recent studies with individuals suffering from events such as rape, combat, loss of a loved one, accidents, natural disasters, etc., have found that 84 to 90 per cent no longer had post-traumatic stress disorder after only three treatment sessions. A recent study financed by Kaiser Permanente revealed that EMDR was twice as effective in half the amount of time compared to the standard traditional care.

The major significance of EMDR is that it allows the brain to heal its psychological problems at the same rate as the rest of the body is healing its physical ailments. Because EMDR allows minds and body to heal at the same rate, it is effectively making time irrelevant in therapy. Given its wide application, EMDR promises to be the therapy of the future.

The previous exercise is a good one for teachers to do with their pupils at the beginning of a new term, or even perhaps once a week. It is quite good fun to do as the children love this kind of activity – you'll probably have to stop because they'll be laughing too much!

What do you now know about eye movements that will assist you in class and as a person?

How will this increase your ability to teach from the front of the room?

What will you do to keep your knowledge of the eye patterns charts current and in your own mind's eye?

Conclusion

Throughout this chapter there have been activities to try and prompts for your reflections. Hopefully you will have tried some of these. Even if you haven't written things down, your deep mind has been working on them for you. Now is a good time to add any more general or specific reflections to your journal that you will be having, and to try out the quiz to reinforce learning. At the back of the book you will find our reflections on the questions. Good luck.

Chapter 2 quiz

	True	False	Maybe
1. Matching and mirroring is simply copying another person's traits, like a monkey			
2. Body language is more truthful than words when it comes to communication			
3. Skin tone, head position, lip size, breathing rate are all conscious communication signals			
4. Can you use changes in voice tones to tell you consistently if a person is happy or not?			
5. People will know immediately if you are matching or mirroring them			
6. We delete pieces of information unconsciously to avoid overwhelm			
7. Eye patterns can tell you where a person has gone to sort information			
8. Knowing how a child's direction filter operates can help in planning behaviour programmes and using rewards or sanctions to motivate behaviour			
9. Some pupils look for similarities and the familiar while others look for differences			
10. You can calibrate on what a person likes/dislikes and apply this to any other situation with this person			
11. The size of the chunks of information that you deliver in the classroom are not important			
12. The NLP three R's are Rapport Reduces Resistance			

Answers and discussion can be found on page 140.

3 The language of life – representational systems

In this chapter we look at

- how people's preferred representational system differs
- ways in which you can ascertain what representational system seems to dominate
- how you can use that information to become a more effective communicator.

The language of life

We all have sensory preferences when we are communicating with others. For some time now the awareness in schools of the different learning styles of children has been gathering momentum. Ideally we all need things presented to us in a variety of ways to give learning the best possible chance to take place. Some of us are very visual people, some prefer auditory, some very tactile, or kinaesthetic. A good communicator will tune in to the preferred communication style by taking note of the representational language and use that as a kind of dialect to enable enhanced communication. This is easy to do once you have raised your awareness of the different styles and learnt how to speak the same dialect as others. You will be amazed at how much more easily you can get your message across and begin to see that everybody has their own personal way of experiencing their universe

So how do we begin to recognize how each person makes sense of this unique world in which they live? One of the easiest ways to discover this is to simply listen to the words that they are using. In NLP, we call this the VAKOG (the representation system), which stands for visual, auditory, kinaesthetic, olfactory, and gustatory. The other system, which also plays a part in this, we call self-talk, the labelling system, or for short, Ai (audio internal).

According to NLP, for many practical purposes the mental processing of events and memories can be treated as if performed by the five senses. For example, Einstein credited his discovery of spacial relativity to a mental visualization of 'sitting on the end of a ray of light', but many people as part of decision making talk to themselves in their heads and won't be making pictures at all. The manner in which this is done, and the effectiveness of the mental strategy employed, play a critical part in the way mental processing takes place. This observation led to the concept of a preferred representational system, the classification of people into fixed visual, auditory or kinaesthetic stereotypes.

This idea was later discredited and dropped within NLP by the early 1980s, in favour of the understanding that most people use all of their senses (whether consciously or unconsciously), and that while one system may seem to dominate, this is often contextualized – globally there is a balance that dynamically varies according to circumstance and mood.

NLP asserts that for most circumstances and most people, four of the five sensory-based modes seem to dominate in mental processing:

- visual thoughts – sight, mental imagery, spatial awareness
- auditory (or linguistic) – sound, speech, dialogue, white noise
- kinaesthetic (or feelings) sense – somatic feelings in the body, temperature, pressure, and also emotion
- self-talk (or audio internal).

The other two senses, gustatory (taste) and olfactory (smell), which are closely associated, often seem to be less significant in general mental processing, and are often considered jointly as one (possibly linked with feelings).

The preferred representational systems have been used for decades and many teachers have observed, and believe, that a student's modality (the words that they use to describe part of the VAKOG), strengths and weaknesses should be considered and that a student learns more when instruction is modified to match preferred modality patterns.

Michael Grinder (1991) has written about learning styles from the NLP point of view in his book *Righting the Educational Conveyor Belt*, giving instructions of how to make the diagnosis with NLP tools such as observing eye movements.

Research on VAKOG

Brockman (1980) experimented with counsellors. One cohort was asked to match representational systems (VAKOG) of their clients and the other counsellors took a more generic, human relations approach to empathizing with their clients.

Results indicated that clients preferred the representational system matching counsellor by a ratio of three to one as opposed to the counsellors using more generic approaches. Although this is only one study, casual observation has indicated that this is an effective way to operate. If you apply the same findings to teaching, it means that your pupils could on a three to one ratio find you empathetic to some degree!

Representational systems are also relevant since some tasks are more optimally performed within one representational system than by another. For example, within education, spelling is better learned by children who have unconsciously used a strategy of visualization, than an unconscious strategy of phonetically 'sounding out' (remember spelling strategies in Chapter 2). When taught to visualize, previously poor spellers can indeed be taught to improve. NLP proponents also found that pacing and leading the various cues tended to build rapport, and allowed people to communicate more effectively. Using similar representational systems to another person can help build rapport.

Skinner and Stephens (2003) explored the use of this model of representational systems in television marketing and communications – and this will be no surprise to many of you, just watch advertisements and notice how the advertising companies have discovered that using all the VAKOG in a short commercial will appeal to a wider audience than using just one or two.

Okay, perhaps it's time for you to discover which system you prefer to use over another. Here's a test for you.

Representational System Preference Test
For each of the following statements, please place a number next to every phrase. Use the following system to indicate your preferences:

  4 = Closest to describing you

  3 = Next best description

  2 = Next best

  1 = Least descriptive of you

  1. I mostly make decisions about money based on:

  - the right gut level feelings ☐
  - which is the best, sound solution and resonates for me ☐
  - after seeing the complete scene in front of me seeing the images in question ☐
  - precise review and study of the situation ☐

2. During an argument, I am most likely to be influenced by:
- the loudness or softness of the other person's tone of voice ☐
- whether or not I can see the other person's viewpoint ☐
- the logic of the other person's argument ☐
- whether or not I am in touch with my own and the other person's feelings ☐

3. I like to be aware of the following in conversation:
- the way people display themselves and give-away facial expressions ☐
- the feelings that we share ☐
- the words I and they choose and whether it all makes good sense ☐
- the variability of sounds and intonations in the 'story' of the voice ☐

4. If I had the choice of these in order, first I would like to:
- find the ideal volume and tuning on a stereo system ☐
- review the layout of the room to understand the person by this method ☐
- select the most comfortable furniture ☐
- look around and take in the décor, pictures and how the room looks before doing anything else ☐

5. Which describes your room that you live in:
- the hi-fi is very prominent and I have an excellent CD/MP3 collection ☐
- it has a practical layout and things are situated in logical locations ☐
- the feel of the place is satisfactory ☐
- the colours you choose and the way a room looks are highest in my values ☐

Step one: Copy your answers above to here:

1.	____K	2.	____A	3.	____V
	____A		____V		____K
	____V		____Ai		____Ai
	____Ai		____K		____A

4.	____A	5.	____A
	____Ai		____Ai
	____K		____K
	____V		____V

Step two: Add the numbers associated with each letter. There are 5 entries for each letter:

	V	A	K	Ai
1				
2				
3				
4				
5				
Totals:				

Step three: The comparison of the total scores in each column will give the relative preference for each of the four major Representational Systems.

The above is a very simple and fun test and gives a generalized indication and is by no means definitive. You would need to do more investigation to validate your results, like the exercise below.

Here is another way of finding out your preferences

If I was to give you the latest, state of the art DVD player with new features on it and it was your responsibility to make it work, would you:
  (A) Grab the manual and read it avidly
  (B) Take the articles out of the box and get to grips with it as you go
  (C) Talk to someone else about setting it up

So, if you answered A, then that's your visual preference, B would be the tactile or kinaesthetic approach and C the auditory way. Again, these are not cast in stone, as they may change in differing contexts.

Favoured Representational Systems

V: Visual

People who are visual often stand or sit with their heads and/or bodies erect, with their eyes up. They will be breathing from the top of their lungs. They often sit forward in their chair and tend to be organized, neat, well-groomed and orderly. They memorize by seeing pictures, and are less distracted by noise. They often have trouble remembering verbal instructions because their minds tend to wander. A visual person will be interested in how your programme **LOOKS**. Appearances are important to them. They are often thin and wiry.

A: Auditory

People who are auditory will move their eyes sideways (remember Richard Nixon?). They breathe from the middle of their chest. They typically talk to themselves, and are easily distracted by noise (some even move their lips when they talk to themselves). They can repeat things back to you easily, they learn by listening, and usually like music and talking on the phone. They memorize by steps, procedures, and sequences (sequentially). The auditory person likes to be TOLD how they're doing, and responds to a certain tone of voice or set of words. They will be interested in what you have to **SAY** about your programme.

K: Kinaesthetic

People who are kinaesthetic will typically be breathing from the bottom of their lungs, so you'll see their stomach go in and out when they breathe. They often move and talk verrry slooowly. They respond to physical rewards, and touching. They also stand closer to people than a visual person. They memorize by doing or 'walking through' something. They will be interested in your programme if it **FEELS RIGHT.**

Ai: Auditory Internal (self-talk)

This person will spend a fair amount of time talking to themselves. They will want to know if your programme **MAKES SENSE**, is it logical, it follows a structure, etc. The auditory digital person can exhibit characteristics of the other major representational systems.

Now you know some of the basics of the VAKOG, how do you think you can apply this knowledge to your lessons?

It's a good thing to know that each individual likes their information in a certain way, whether they have good or bad experiences coupled with a certain VAKOG modality.

Some children can happily sit and listen for a long time, while others love to look at pictures to get good information. For some, neither of these learning styles will work. For those, they would have to try it out, use it, physically touch the subject, or even dance it!

This is well known in the business sales marketing whereby the salesperson (if they have been well trained) will find out which modality is your favourite, and then sell to you in that way. If you were interested in a car for instance, and they find out your favoured modality is tactile (kinaesthetic), they will get you to actually test drive the car!

Ideas for reflection

What have you learned about the different ways people represent their world? For instance, if a pupil tells you that they just can't grasp the information or that they don't feel good about a subject, what could you do for improved connection with them?

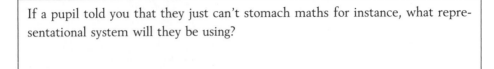

If a pupil told you that they just can't stomach maths for instance, what representational system will they be using?

If someone told you that they can't see the point of physical exercise and that they just don't get the picture, what will they be doing inside?

For your interest, here is some further research into the VAKOG which you can peruse if you wish.

Why should you believe this?

You may be forgiven for reading this and disagreeing, however, Bandler and Grinder (1976) suggested that people represent and organize the external world using internal systems based on the five senses. They also posited that the language, or words selected and favoured when describing their perspective, give us an insight into their consciousness. They called this the predicate. The most important implication of this model was that by consciously selecting your predicates to match those of the person with whom you want to communicate, you may be more effective in accomplishing clearer and more direct communication.

Elich, Thompson and Miller (1985) suggest we have a preferred system and process visually, kinaesthetically or aurally. Consequently it could be that communication between two people, for example teacher and pupil, or as the authors noted, therapist and client, could be difficult if they do not share the same preferred system, and we have already discussed Brockman's findings (1980). However, Ellickson (1983) suggested that if we can identify the other person's representational system and learn to communicate using the same sensory system, then communication is enhanced through improved rapport. An obvious corollary is that improved rapport and communication will lead to improved learning.

Einspruch and Forman (1985) seem to be the only researchers who took note of the rather implicit suggestions made by Bandler and Grinder, criticizing numerous research studies for apparently not considering or providing adequate controls to test the effect of context in influencing the system used. It needs to be borne in mind that, as with calibrating on behaviour, so we have to calibrate on language and work out how people see the use of certain words. Using primary representational systems is an art not a science. Whatever academic arguments exist around the finer points in practice, awareness and judicious use of a person's PRS does pay dividends.

Activity

Ascertaining representational system language in your pupils – Can you see, hear and feel what I mean?

A, B and C

A asks B the following questions. Both A and C listen clearly for all sensory language used by your B, and write each one down as they say it. You will notice that there are essentially four questions, but after each one I have added an extra question to try to draw out more thinking. Sometimes, because of the falseness of the situation, it is hard for people to free up on the answers, so asking the extra questions stated here will help them to keep talking without you putting words into their mouth.

B – forget about what you are doing and try to answer the questions as naturally and honestly and deeply and congruently as you can. Close your eyes if it will help you.

1. This morning how did you make up your mind what clothes to wear today?
2. Is there anything else you do?
3. Tell me, why you do your favourite hobby?
4. Yes, tell me a bit more about that.
5. When you are really tired, how do you motivate yourself to get up in the morning?
6. Do you do anything else?
7. How do you know when it's time to take a break and do something that is fun?
8. Do you do that every time, or do you sometimes do something else?

Remember, you are not interested in the actual answers. The context is irrelevant. Just listen carefully for language that indicates visual, auditory or kinaesthetic, or auditory internal, preferences. All you are looking for here is to see where your B goes to find the information you have requested. Change roles and each have a turn in each position. Look at the predominant language style. Use the tables below to help you to decode further.

Categorization of words in Representational System

Using the tables below you can start to ascertain the preferred representational styles of anyone you have observed. The tables of words and phrases below give an idea of how to categorize words into representational systems. You may not agree with all of them, but you will see a pattern emerging as you read through. You may also feel more in tune with one column than others. Have a read through and find out.

Visual	Auditory	Kinaesthetic	Auditory Internal
Memorize by seeing pictures and are less distracted by noise. Often have trouble remembering and are bored by long verbal instructions because their mind may wander. They are interested by how the programme looks.	Typically are easily distracted by noise. They can repeat things back to you easily and learn by listening. They like music and like to talk on the phone. Tone of voice and the words used can be important.	Often they talk slowly and breathily. They respond to physical rewards and touching. They memorize by doing or walking through something. They will be interested in a programme that feels right or gives them a gut feeling.	They spend a fair amount of time talking to themselves. They memorize by steps, procedures, sequences. They will want to know the programme makes sense. They can also sometimes exhibit characteristics of other representational systems.
Attractive	Argue	Bend	Change
Blurred	Ask	Bounce	Conceive
Bright	Call	Break	Consider
Cloudy	Chatter	Brush	Decide
Colourful	Complain	Burdened	Distinct
Conceal	Crescendo	Carry	Experience
Enlighten	Cry	Clumsy	Insensitive
Expose	Discuss	Comfortable	Know
Eyed	Echo	Concrete	Learn

Foggy	Explain	Cowering	Motivate
Glance	Growl	Crouching	Perceive
Glimpse	Gurgling	Exciting	Process
Glitzy	Harmonize	Hurt	Sense
Graphic	Hear	Immovable	Think
Hazy	Hum	Movement	Understand
Illuminate	Lecture	Numb	
Look	Melodious	Pressure	
Obscure	Mumble	Pull	
Observe	Noisy	Push	
Peer	Outspoken	Scrape	
Perspective	Overtones	Shaky	
Preview	Quiet	Slip	
Reflect	Resonance	Smooth	
See	Sang	Solid	
Staring	Screaming	Spiky	
Twinkle	Shout	Stuffed	
View	Shriek	Sweep	
Visualize	Shrill	Thick	
	Silent	Touchy	
	Sounds	Trample	
	Tell	Twist	
	Translate	Unmoving	
	Undertones	Unfeeling	
	Unhearing	Wash	
	Utter	Weigh	
	Vocal		

Sensory Predicate Phrases

Auditory	Kinaesthetic	Visual
A little bird told me	All washed up	An eyeful
All ears	An uphill climb	Appears to me
An earful	Boils down to	Bird's eye view
Be heard	Catch my drift	Catch a glimpse of
Blabber mouth	Catch on	Clear-cut
Call on	Chip off the old block	Clear image
Clear as a bell	Come to grips with	Clear view
Clearly expressed	Connect with	Crystal clear
Describe in sound detail	Control yourself	Eye to eye
Express yourself soundly	Cool/calm/collected	Flashed on
Give a vocal account	Firm foundations	Get a perspective
Give me your ear	Floating on air	Get a scope on
Grant me a telling audience	Get a handle on	Hazy idea
Heard voices	Get a hold of	Horse of a different colour
Hidden messages	Get a load of this	I get the picture
Hold your tongue	Get in touch with	In light of
Idle talk	Get the creeps	In person
I hear you	Hand in hand	In view of
Inquire soundly into	Hang in there	I see what you mean
Loud and clear	Heated argument	Looks good to me
Make music	Hold it	Make a scene
Outspoken	I catch your drift	Mental picture
Power of speech	It feels right to me	Mind's eye
Purrs like a kitten	Make contact	Paint a picture
Rings a bell	Pain in the neck	Photographic
State your purpose	Plain sailing	Plainly seen
Say something simple	Pull some strings	Pretty as a picture

That rings a bell	Sharp as a tack	See to it
That resonates	Slipped my mind	Short sighted
To tell the truth	Smooth operator	Showing off
Tune in/tune out	Start from scratch	Sight for sore eyes
Unheard of	Tap into	Take a dim view
Utterly	Touch on	Take a look
Voice an opinion	Treading on thin ice	Tunnel vision
Wish you could hear me now	Walk through	Wide eyed

Translation between representational styles

Each of the representational 'languages' can be translated into the others. Look at the sentences below and see how differently the same situation can be matched using the same representational style, and how they can be described in different representational styles.

Example 1   My future looks hazy

Match: **Visual:** When I look to the future, it doesn't seem clear.

Translate: **Auditory:** I can't tune in to my future.

Kinesthetic: I can't get a feel for what seems to be going to happen.

Example 2   Sarah doesn't listen to me

Match: **Auditory:** Sarah goes deaf when I talk.

Translate: **Visual:** Sarah never sees me, even when I'm right in front of her eyes.

Kinesthetic: I get the feeling Sarah doesn't care to even try to catch my drift.

Example 3   Mary gets churned up inside when the head expects her assignment

Match: **Kinesthetic:** Mary gets agitated and tense over submitting her assignment.

Translate: **Visual:** Mary goes blind crazy and her vision fogs up when her assignment becomes due.

Auditory: Mary's ears ring because she has to face the music if her assignment isn't in on time.

Idea to look at

Choose a child you work with and listen to the types of words they use. You will notice they will probably use all types of the visual, auditory and kinaesthetic words but one type will usually predominate. Then practise translating your language to their system.

If they say 'I don't *see* what you mean', don't say 'Let me repeat it', instead say 'Let me *show* you what I mean'. Then perhaps use an image or a pictorial example.

If they say 'What you're saying doesn't *feel* right to me', don't say 'Take a different view', instead say 'Let's *move* through these points another way'. Then use an example that means they have to move their body to understand it. If it were a geography lesson, for instance, you'd get them to walk around the classroom as if it were a globe and work with the pupil that way.

Keep practising and make a note of what you have done to reinforce your learning. You will become more and more aware of how other people think, and more flexible in how you respond. Remember to employ all of your NLP skills that you have read about and practised – build rapport, match and mirror, get the trust of the parent.

Reflections on translating your language to the system of a child in your class.

Summary

- When people are like each other they like each other.

- When you like someone, you are willing to assist them to get what they want. Most communication is outside our conscious awareness.

- As a master communicator you will communicate best with people when you employ *their* preferred ways of speaking.

- If you are working with someone who is in high visual, sit up in your chair, breath from the top of your lungs – within reason!

- If you are with someone who is auditory, slow down a bit, modulate your voice more and listen, really listen.

- If they are kinaesthetic, slow waaaay doooown. Talk to them about feelings. Change your pace so that it matches theirs, and really get a feel for what they are communicating.

- You will know when you are in rapport, you will feel congruent, movements will mirror and match – you can begin to lead and they will follow your movements, you may feel a sense of warmth and they may feel they have known you all their life.

Chapter 3 quiz

	True	False	Maybe
1. Students learn more when instructed in styles different from their own representational style			
2. Knowing your own representational style (VAKOG) will help you to modify your communication to match that of your pupils			
3. You can 'translate' from your language to that of another person by emulating their representational style			
4. If you are working with a child who is highly visual, slow down and modulate your voice more and really listen well			
5. When working with someone who is kinaesthetic, sit up high in your chair, breathe from the top of your lungs			
6. When you gain rapport you experience a sense of knowing the other person.			
7. To practise rapport skills choose a child in your class you get on really well with and match and mirror their mannerisms with respect			

8. Simply changing the timbre of your voice can be enough to establish good rapport			
9. You cannot build rapport with a whole class			
10. It is impossible to tell from a person's eye movements what they are thinking			
11. EMDR is a technique used to link different areas of the brain			

Answers and discussion can be found on page 141.

4 Anchoring, reframing, and metaphor

Three very useful NLP techniques explained – anchoring, reframing, and metaphor

In this chapter you are going to be introduced to three of the key NLP techniques, which you are likely to find useful in your classroom. They are quite different techniques used for different applications, but each is quite simple, and extremely useful in everyday life and in classroom life – everyone benefits.

Anchoring in the classroom

Have you wondered why you like certain foods, drinks, people, and not others?

How come some people have a terrible association with heights and others with spiders?

In NLP we call this anchoring. Anchoring happens when an emotional state is so strongly associated with a stimulus, that the object or event is associated with that state from then on.

Activity to try out

Do a thought experiment to explore this further. This exercise is about your inner world and how it can connect to your feelings, emotions and behaviour. All you need to do to begin is to relax and go inside. So, we can try something together, and this little experiment will allow you to have access to the states for learning that you want your children to have access to.

Do it and see what happens!

Wherever you are, get in touch with a really good experience that you've had. As you are inside this experience, notice what's special about it. What is it that is making such a beautiful experience? And allow yourself to drift into this and find something that is so enjoyable that you just get taken away with it.

So now you're really inside this experience, and don't have any judgement on it, it's absolutely just the one that your deep mind came up with and it will be the perfect one. That's right, now allow yourself to be inside this experience, and inside the feelings and the pictures and sounds. If you are still reading this page perhaps you haven't gone away with it so much as you could! Allow yourself to drift away into this experience and really experience what it's like being you in that situation.

Okay, come back! (Some of you may not want to!)

Now, next thing, when you're really feeling this experience as strongly as you possibly can, or see the pictures as much as you possibly can, bring in an object, a metaphor or anything to identify/associate with this experience – it might be a ruler on the table or it might be a finger of your hand or maybe you touch a shirt in a certain way. Maybe you just look out of the window of your room as you remember this internal experience. Okay?

If you need to do this again, go ahead now that you have all the instructions here before you start. Please go ahead and this time really drift away and get inside this experience, this beautiful experience. When the state is peaking, at the same time make an association with something in your room or make a picture so as to remember this state. It may even be a word that you might say in your head at the same time as experiencing your peak state.

Okay, so now, if you've done this experiment correctly, what you'll find is that the two things (the state inside and the thing you associated with it) are now linked with each other. This is what we now call your anchor, so it might be the shirt you touched, the window you looked out of, the picture you have in your mind.

You can test this now. Just bring back that visual image or touch your shirt in that particular way. Or was it the way you looked out of the window while having the good state?

So go ahead and test the anchor. Now, you may find that the experience is not 100 per cent of the intensity of the original state, like when you were really drifting away inside it, yet you may find there is enough energy in there to give your body a sense of the chemical reaction, the nice feelings that were associated there.

So anywhere between 50 to 100 per cent of the original intensity will work perfectly. What this means is that, as long as the environment is okay for you, you can bring back this experience whenever you choose to do so, in whatever situation, and use it to your advantage.

How did that feel?

In NLP we learn not only to access internal resources and states of mind but also to literally anchor them to a specific stimulus. In a way anchoring is a form of Pavlovian conditioning for people. The amazing thing is that with skill (and consistency), anchors can not only affect you, but also the children, parents, and colleagues around you.

In this chapter we will allocate a variety of techniques that can help you with learning and motivational states, and organize your classroom environment from your inner mind out, rather like a director on a film set.

Anchoring from Pavlov (woof)

You will no doubt have heard about the scientist Ivan Petrovich Pavlov (1849–1936). He was a Russian physiologist, psychologist, and physician who was awarded the Nobel Prize in Physiology of Medicine in 1904 for research pertaining to the digestive system. Pavlov is widely known for first describing the phenomenon of classical conditioning.

He was born in Ryazan where his father worked as the village priest.

He began his higher education as a student at the Ryazan Ecclesiastical Seminary, but then dropped out and enrolled at the University of Saint Petersburg to study the natural sciences. He received his doctorate in 1879.

In the1890s Pavlov was investigating the gastric function of dogs by externalizing a salivary gland so he could collect, measure and analyse the saliva and what response it had to food under different conditions. He noticed that the dogs tended to salivate before food coated with chilli powder was actually delivered to their mouths, and set out to investigate this 'psychic secretion', as he called it. He decided that this was more interesting than the chemistry of saliva, and changed the focus of his research, carrying out a long series of experiments in which he manipulated the stimuli occurring before the presentation of food. He thereby established the basic laws for the establishment of what he called 'conditional reflexes' – that is, reflex responses, like salivation, that only occurred conditionally upon specific previous experiences of the animal. These experiments were carried out in the 1890s and 1900s and were known to Western scientists through translations of individual accounts, but first became fully available in English in a book published in 1927.

In NLP, we understand that we can create a conditioned response, and not only to a reflex but also to an emotional state (such as confidence, enthusiasm, calmness). How useful would it be to be able to instantly call upon a particular emotional state to aid you in your teaching or the children in their learning?

Anchoring is one of the most useful of NLP techniques. Anchoring is the process by which a memory, a feeling, or some other response is associated with (or anchored to) something else.

Pleasure or anger are natural processes that usually occur without our awareness. For example, when you were young you undoubtedly participated in family activities that gave you great pleasure. The pleasure was associated with the activity itself, so when you think of the activity, or are reminded of it, you will tend to really experience some pleasurable feelings. By the same process of associated memory anchors are reactivated or triggered.

So, for instance, let's say you have a child who at a very early age at the beginning of their learning cycles has been told (not by you of course!) very negative things about themselves and about their ability to learn. Think back to the example of the dogs, and the food. If in any learning experience provided to a child when they are in a highly intense state negative comments (which will be experienced as a command by a young mind) are given, such as *'You are stupid'*, or *'You just don't learn'*, or *'You'll never do this'*, the child will begin to associate learning with themselves being stupid, having little ability, etc.

> Think back to your own learning experiences. Which of the subjects did you really, really enjoy? Think back to your earliest memories of how this came about, who were the teachers, what was happening in the classroom?

Most probability you had a good teacher or a good state was present when the subjects you enjoyed most were presented to you, so it's not just that you were a bright child, it's also very much about the environment. The environment was conducive to learning and to make you feel good about learning. Therefore, when you approach the subject, the same state is there for you. Then this reframes the notion of just being a great learner, it's more about what atmosphere was present at the onset of learning.

Here's another example about anchoring in learning states. One thing I've noticed more than anything about computer repairers is that it's not about how bright or intelligent they are with the mechanics of the computer, it's just that they really enjoy the process of tinkering. Perhaps with most of the rest of us, the very thought of going inside the computer and even sometimes the software turns our stomachs over and we just push it away and give the task to somebody else.

So it's not really that they are so intelligent or so bright with computers, it's just the fact that they have a good state when they think about the process of the internal mechanics of computers. In other words, they simply have had good associations when approaching the whole subject. Also they may well have a good recovery strategy when things don't go well, so that they still have a good state even in adversity!

Some of the other factors to take into consideration here are the different ways that people like to learn. If a pupil has had pleasurable experiences and stores them visually, then that's how they will like their information when they come to learn new things. Some will have had very good associations with kinaesthetics so they will want to have that somewhere in their learning cycles. Some others love sounds, so they want to hear the sound of the subject or hear the teacher talk about the subject in a certain way, or even hear an audio book for instance.

All these things have to be put into the equation by you the teacher when you're standing in front of a class. So how do you do this? How do you satisfy all of these different learning styles, all of these different minds in a Pavlovian way that will satisfy the majority of your classroom? What about pupils who have no access to *any* good learning experiences, how will you get them to learn new excellent strategies for good states in learning?

So this section really is about heightening your consciousness around what you are doing and what you are anchoring when you're in front of a room full of people with differing abilities.

What anchors are you already using in your work with children?

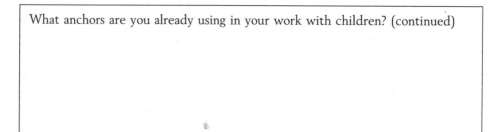

What anchors are you already using in your work with children? (continued)

Visual anchors

You can use visual anchors to anchor the resourceful state. You can use external or internal anchors. For example, you could use a figure on a bracelet to anchor being calm and relaxed. The external anchor always has to be there for you to use. You may find it relaxing and calming to view a certain landscape but, unless you can carry it around with you, it is of limited value. You can, however, use an internal image of the landscape to anchor your resourceful feeling.

Some examples of visual anchors are:

- Symbols. For example, you could use a circle as a symbol for being calm and relaxed and anchor this to your excellent state from earlier.

- People, such as a trusted friend or mentor ... or even a person from history or current affairs, as long as they evoke your excellent state.

- Various objects and landscapes can be used as anchors for being calm and relaxed. For example, you could imagine:
  - a favourite place
  - a flower you remember for its qualities
  - a river taking away stress and bringing love.

Are you getting the picture?

Auditory anchors

You can use a sound as an anchor. Like the visual anchors, sounds can be internal or external. Songs are anchors. Mozart has been used for enhancing learning, but any song can be used; sometimes using a particular tune to bring the class back into the room after a break can rapidly put them into a learning state. For an internal audio, you could even hear your own voice telling you something good and relaxing.

You can think of a movie and its soundtrack; there are so many ways of getting yourself tuned in!

Here are some things you can hear and remember:

- the sound of running water to relax or stimulate

- bells to energize (you can use real bells in the classroom (no, not Notre Dame!)

- classical music for you and/or for the pupils to aid relaxation and therefore learning

- music which tells your pupils what's coming next (like to come back from doing something you have given them to do . . . saves your voice and is more fun!).

Kinaesthetic anchors

Examples of kinaesthetic anchors are:

- Making a circle with the second finger and the thumb to relax (put some relaxing thoughts in there before the day starts).

- Touching yourself on the hand or knuckle. You can choose a point and treat it like an acupressure point – pressing on it to fire the required excellent state.

- Having a really comfortable chair, or making it really comfortable, so you feel like the king or queen when you sit down!

- Wearing clothes that you feel perfect in . . . make the effort!

How to use anchors in the classroom

So, from what you've heard so far, what do you think is the most important thing to be able to do as the teacher in a classroom full of people so as to create a good environment? Of course the right state is the most important thing of all!

How is it to have a room full of hungry children salivating at the prospect of learning?

What is it like when you walk into the room, stand and say certain key phrases in certain places and get immediate attention? Or have certain visuals/sounds so that immediately the pupils turn on to the prospect of having a really good session with you?

Perhaps this already happens for you, or perhaps you think this is out of reach for you? Well, from my experience of teaching up to 50 people at a time in many different environments in many different situations, it's very possible! I have had to deliver information to children who are not allowed to go into mainstream schools, because they cause too much trouble and aggravation. I can tell you from first-hand experience that all of this is possible and all of this will make your day so much brighter, so much more enjoyable, so much more human!

So let's start with your own state so you can get a first-hand experience of a good frame of mind, because that's where it all starts. What's in your mind, what's in your body, what's in your sight when you immediately walk into a classroom?

If you really intend that your children, your pupils, can have a good experience with you then you must start with a good experience inside of yourself. It's too much to ask somebody else to do all the work to have a good learning experience and feel good when you do not do so yourself!

For instance, just before walking into your classroom at the beginning of the day have your anchor or anchors ready and set them off as you walk into your classroom.

What, exactly, is the kind of state you'd like to have? Of course this may take a little time to set up with yourself, because if you've got all the negative anchors inside your learning environment you'll need to collapse them or remove these old negative anchors before you can install new ones. You may start with one area of your classroom, your desk for instance, and have a really good positive anchor around there.

Some people use pictures of the family as an anchor on the desk. As long as whatever you have associated to does give you really good feelings, then these will work.

Okay, so far we have set up the anchors for you. Now let's look at how we can project these anchors out for your pupils.

If you have grasped the basic concepts here, you can begin to realize that your state is what controls a room. It's the same for actors. A certain actor will influence the whole nature of a film. So wherever you go in the classroom, your state will determine what's associated there with you. Your amount of consciousness will then dictate how well you are doing with your anchors!

Some of you by now may be thinking, 'gosh, I have to be a teacher, a mother/father, a wife/husband *and* an actor now!!!' Well, yes and no. You see, you already have set up the anchors in your classroom just by being there and doing what you've done. All that's happening now is that you are becoming more aware of what you are doing and how to get the results that *you'd* like!

Okay, so think of a film set and all the places on the stage that are your classroom. Think of all the different states you'd like your pupils to have: creativity, learning, quietness, teamwork, individual work, extrovert, introvert, whatever it is you require as the state for the class. Now see where/how you can divide up the classroom like a film set and notice where you'd like to anchor the states. In acting or training circles, these are called stage anchors. For instance, if you'd like the particular state of learning or creativity, then what you would do is go to the particular places in the classroom you have decided will be right for this and which would evoke creativity or learning. As long as you have got the general experience or the general atmosphere of creativity (for instance, while telling a story), your pupils will become very interested and very tuned in to you in this particular place. Whenever you go back there again, and use the same kind of voice or words which are associated with this feeling, then your pupils will immediately go back there with you into that space when you need them to.

Similarly, if you want to allow them to have a place in the classroom that can be used for dealing with upsets or with complaints that pupils may have, or even aggression, you can set this up as well. Make it well away from the creativity place! So mark out where it may be, like a dumping place, so that whenever an upset occurs, you deal with it there. So, in this case, you would deliberately have walked to that place in the classroom if there happened to be a problem in the room. You can then return to another place for your next piece.

So, by changing the areas that relate to different states, you'll be able to manage the energy of the room and manage what you want the pupils to be listening to and looking at much more effectively than before.

This is no different from the way Pavlov experienced dogs responding to anything that was present when they were in a highly motivated or intense state. The only difference here is that you are substituting the bell for specific places in the classroom.

So, what you have to do with your pupils is to make them hungry for whatever you are teaching and then anchor that with a specific voice, or in a specific place in the room that you choose and they will automatically remember next time you introduce that voice or place or picture. Then you'll be able to move through the day with much more control.

So what happens if you are not in a good state of mind? Well, if you're not feeling particularly good one day, this is where the anchors come in really handy as well. Because the anchors are already set up and the children expect certain things from certain areas of the room, you might well achieve 50 per cent or 75 per cent effectiveness and still have a great day with the pupils! You just use the anchors you've set up on day one and the anchors will do the rest for you!

If you imagine your favourite comedian, or even your favourite TV personality, sometimes just by coming onto the stage you feel different and they seem to change your own state. They don't even have to say anything. You associate them with certain attributes of humour or abilities and then they just have to hint at what you already know about them and you are already laughing out loud or transfixed by their presence.

Okay, now that you have the basics of anchoring along with the consequent possibilities for yourself in your environment, you can use this in a more advanced way. Think of multiple, really good events which have happened in your life and place them in your favourite spot inside your classroom, alternatively you can touch a knuckle of your own as you think of one event after another. Remember to allow yourself to drift into or powerfully engage with these memories which are about what you love to do, how you love to do it and who you love to do it with. Then, as you are at the peak of those states, as you're really intensely feeling or imagining these things happening, touch your knuckle or associate this to an object in your classroom that you can easily have access to at any time. What will happen is that this resource of yours will grow more and more powerful. And you can keep adding to this area of this knuckle if something really good happens in the classroom or outside the classroom. So what you will end up with is a highly stimulating, motivating, powerful resource anchor – right on your knuckle!

If you want to do this on an area of the floor in your classroom, imagine that there's a spotlight above you beaming down onto a stage. You can get into one of these memories and drift into/associate into what you really love to do, and with whom, and step into the spotlight when the feeling is really intense. When you feel this feeling just coming off slightly, step back out of the spotlight. Now repeat what you have done. When another state or another thing you really love to do starts coming out and you can really feel it, step inside the spotlight area again. Then, when you have done perhaps three, or even five of the states, step outside, shake your hands out just to break the intensity and then test this resource anchor by stepping inside the spotlight area again.

What should happen is that you now find you have access to multiple good states, just by walking into that area!

Being very flexible as you are, you could actually move the spotlight around the classroom whenever you need it. You could even take the spotlight, shrink it down and keep a miniature version in your pocket and take it wherever you go; to a presentation, to a meeting, to a relationship and just turn it on when you need it!

The most important thing about doing these exercises for yourself is that you make that time to really fully associate into each of these memories before you do the anchoring. If you do that, then they'll work every time.

Collapsing anchors

Okay, now here's how to use anchors to be able to dismiss old negative events or feelings. The purpose of eliciting certain responses is to establish a more favourable receptive ground for communicating your messages effectively.

The person's state of mind, their feelings – the things they are attending to (both consciously and unconsciously) – will be of critical significance with regard to how they receive your ideas and suggestions. By eliciting the kind of responses you want when you present your idea, you increase the chances of having your idea favourably received and acted on. This will come as no surprise to anyone who has ever tried selling, but even the most sophisticated salesperson often ignores this basic fact.

Here is an example of how to deal with a negative situation using anchors.

Pupil: Miss Jones, I am really worried that I won't pass, because I get nervous, every time I think of the exams.

Teacher: Okay, Henrietta, but first, let me ask you, what do you love about school? What do you love about learning?

Pupil: I really like sports miss, that's something I really like!

Teacher: What is it you like about sports, Henrietta?

Pupil: I love just running around, I feel really completely charged up and excited!

(At this point, the teacher notices, if the pupil is in an intense, highly motivated state)

Teacher: As you think about running around being completely charged up and excited, what would it be like to be fully engaged in the exams, running through them as eagerly as you running in sports, now!

The teacher will now notice what is happening. If the pupil looks engaged in this idea, and she is running through the process, then things will be changing. Just by having the pupil change her state while thinking about the old problem will make a difference!

You can then test the anchors by asking her whether there is now anything different regarding how she feels about the exams. If there is still nervousness there, then you need to apply another anchor or more anchors until the state is so good that she experiences the very positive state she feels when running, and combining/associating the state with the exams, the negative state will disappear into a very good state.

Here is another example of how to deal with a negative situation using anchors.

Pupil: Miss Smith, I don't feel good about maths.

Teacher: Peter, let me ask you first, what is one of your favourite superheroes?

Pupil: Well I really love the X-Men.

Teacher: What is it about the X-Men, you really love?

Pupil: Well, they are smart and they are strong.

Teacher: In what areas of life are you smart and strong?

Pupil: I am very good at fixing bicycles!

Teacher: As you think of you fixing bicycles, let yourself have a good feeling about that now, and perhaps even allow an image to arrive in your mind about you doing it successfully.

(Teacher notices if that pupil goes into a good state. If not, talk to the limit more about what they love or what is good about them fixing the bicycle)

Teacher: Now, Peter, as you think about that and the resources you have, imagine yourself in the classroom considering maths. As you also consider fixing your bike, and being resourceful and the various ways you have to approaching the topic of maths, perhaps you can think about how would you approach a problem with a bike? Now, how do you feel differently about maths?

(Teacher again notices to see whether pupil is still in a good state when considering maths. If not, the resource anchor is not yet strong enough. So they will need to attach more resources before considering maths and collapsing that old anchor)

Okay, let's recap on anchoring.

1. You can take powerful states that are inside you and move them to any object, time or place.

2. You can get into states and transfer them to others so they can experience them for themselves; you can do this via metaphors, anecdotes or your passion for using language skilfully.

3. The more you bring up powerful states and place them on objects or yourself (for instance a knuckle, finger or shirt cuff), the more these states can build and multiply the strength.

4. If you, or a pupil, are not in a good state, you can access their own anchors by asking them what they love in their life. When you see them inside that state, you can introduce the negative state and it should disappear.

5. Make your classroom like a film set, with stage anchors all around. Plan it before your day starts (you can use the goal-setting idea in this chapter).

Journal questions for you to think about

- How do I feel about setting up work in the classroom right now?
- Are there any areas in my classroom that I would like to change or anchor?
- How will I change them?
- When will I do that?
- Who else will I tell about this to make it more exciting?

This last question is very important because the more you share motivation and new ways of doing things, the more it reenforces your good work. Just make sure it's the right person to talk to!

Reframing with children and young people

The content or meaning of a situation is determined by what you choose to focus on. For example, a huge electricity power failure can be seen as disruptive, given all you have to get done. It can just as easily (as far as your limitations of your nervous system are concerned) be viewed as an opportunity to spend time doing other things. If you are at home, then perhaps some intimate time with your partner, or if you are at school maybe to have fun with the children by finding innovative ways to manage the situation!

A content reframe is useful for statements such as: 'I get annoyed when my teacher stands behind me while I am working.' Notice how the person has taken the situation and given it a specific meaning – which may or may not be true – and in so doing limits her resourcefulness and possible courses of action. To reframe this situation, remember the NLP presupposition *every behaviour has a positive intention* and ask yourself questions such as:

- What other meaning could the teacher's behaviour have? Or for what purpose does she do it? A possible reframe might be: 'Is it possible she wants to help and does not know how to offer her assistance in any other way?'

- What is the positive value in this behaviour? The positive value could be related to the teacher's behaviour (as above) or it could be related to the speaker's behaviour. A possible reframe to a child who states this might be: 'Isn't it great that you know your boundaries and are not prepared to allow someone else to cross them?'

One fact to keep in mind is that memories are not exactly true. To demonstrate, let's look again at the NLP presupposition: 'A map is not the territory' and 'the menu is not the meal'.

The map is not the territory is a statement made by Alfred Korzybski (1931), encapsulating his view that an abstraction derived from something, or a reaction to it, is not the thing itself, for example, the pain from a stone falling on your foot is not the stone; one's opinion of a child, favourable or unfavourable, is not that child; a metaphorical representation of a concept is not the concept itself; and so on.

The Belgian surrealist artist René Magritte illustrated the concept with the statement 'perception always intercedes between reality and ourselves'. He demonstrates this in a number of paintings including a famous work entitled *The Treachery Of Images*, which consists of a drawing of a pipe with the caption, Ceci n'est pas une pipe (This is not a pipe). The test would be to attempt to smoke it (yes, there will be some smoke, yet it would be the type a fire extinguisher would be called for).

A specific abstraction or reaction does not capture all facets of its source: the pain in your foot does not convey the internal structure of the stone, you don't know everything that is going on in the life of a child or their mind, etc., and thus may limit an individual's understanding and cognitive abilities unless the two are distinguished. Korzybski held that many people do confuse maps with territories, in this sense. Therefore even a memory is not whole and complete when you consider all the possible variations of a single event and all the possible meanings you could put on that event.

So when you view your class and people in it, it's just a measurement of the capability of your own mind really. How you 'interpret' the events in your own class and whatever happens is constructed and held in reality by yourself! Some of you may not like how you do that, yet at least this knowledge may give you a more 'real' picture than you had before.

Here are some examples of reframing.

> During the 1984 campaign for the US presidency, there was considerable concern about Ronald Reagan's age. Speaking during the presidential debate with Walter Mondale, Reagan said 'I will not make age an issue of this campaign. I am not going to exploit, for political purposes, my opponent's youth and inexperience.' Reagan's age was not an issue for the remainder of the campaign!

> There is a story about Thomas Watson Sr, the first President of IBM. A young worker had made a mistake that lost IBM $1 million of business. She was called in to the President's office and as she walked in said, 'Well, I guess you have called me here to fire me.' 'Fire you?', Mr Watson replied, 'I just spent $1 million on your education!'

As you can see, events can be turned any which way up to make meanings 'feel' differently, even though they are the same events!

Even meaning itself can be reframed. In order to compile dictionaries, the process is to scour the world for words and notice what context they appear in. Depending on the *context*, plus *difinitio per genus proximum et differentia specifica* (definition by nearest kind or specific differences), that's the meaning that subsequently will be attributed to that word.

So even meaning is context dependent! In the extreme, think of someone coming to work in their underwear and the feelings people would have towards that. Now imagine the same person on a beach or in a bathroom. Perhaps even more accurately a nightclub! All that has changed is the context (yes, I know wearing underwear on a beach isn't too popular!).

Here's another example of reframing and how it can change meaning. This is a true story of one father (who was a very successful businessman) who brought his daughter in to see one of our trainers complaining bitterly that his daughter did not listen to him, was unruly and 'too headstrong'. Our trainer looked calmly at the father, the daughter, then the father again and responded: 'I imagine that you run your own business in a very definite, headstrong way, yes?' The father looked a little shocked and nodded his head, almost involuntarily. 'Well, isn't it refreshing to know that you have brought your daughter up to be just as successful as yourself, and in the future perhaps notice how incredibly successful she will be with this attitude!' The father almost jumped backwards with the unexpected realization that confronted him. He left almost immediately, having seen the situation in a different light!

Of course, you will need a lot of rapport to be able to deliver communication like that, yet our aim is that you'll develop these powerful tools as you progress through this book or undertake training for yourself.

Children and teaching

Children exhibit all sorts of behaviours – some appropriate and some not so appropriate. Focusing mainly on a child's inappropriate behaviours is very likely to result in the child feeling overly criticized or attacked, resulting in an increase in problem behaviour or the child becoming overly defensive. As an alternative, a teacher may choose two courses of action:

- Assuming *'every behaviour has a positive intention'*, the teacher may choose to discover the positive intention. Then the teacher can discuss with the child other behaviours that would meet both the teacher's and the child's needs.
- The teacher may point out where or in what context that type of behaviour is acceptable; thus validating to the child that his behaviours are useful in certain contexts.

Reframing yourself

Here are two examples of reframing yourself from the above presupposition 'Every behaviour is appropriate in some context' (and therefore has a positive intent).

John has a diagnosis for ADHD and keeps shouting out and being too loud. What's one positive intent you can notice here? Okay, so his positive intent may be to keep himself interested, to keep his energy levels up so he can fully engage with the class. Whether this is 'true' or not, it's possible to fully interpret his actions that way. So what's your response?

If you want an extreme version, get him up in front of the class to do something: sing a song, do a dance, talk to the class. If you don't think that would work, use his energy to make your energy even better: out-energy him! Another course would be to make him responsible for something that is happening in class: perhaps he can be responsible for making sure everyone has pens and writing paper, or anything else you can think of to use his energy and sense of attention well.

Another example may be an unhappy girl, making sultry and disruptive comments during class. What could be the positive intent here? Well, it could be (and most probably is) that she is unhappy with something in life and cannot get rid of it. We can all relate to that, can't we? So instead of berating her, which wouldn't help matters at all, you could ask her to tell you what's going on. To make this work, you would have to be truly interested in what she has to say. Hopefully you won't get an answer like Vicky Pollard would give, yet even if you do, it's something!

When she eventually lets on to what's going on behind the scenes you'll have something to reframe.

Activity for you – reframing the diagnostic criteria for ADHD

Below are some of the diagnostic criteria for Attention Deficit Hyperactivity Disorder. Try to take one of them and reframe it in a positive way. For example, the first one could be reframed as 'good at seeing the whole picture without being held back by detail'.

- Often fails to give close attention to details.
- Is often easily distracted by extraneous stimuli.
- Often fidgets with hands or feet or squirms in seat.
- Often runs about or climbs excessively in situations in which it is inappropriate.
- Is often 'on the go' or often acts as if 'driven by a motor'.

ADHD reframe

You could also do a similar activity for other conditions like Asperger's syndrome. All personality types have their good sides as well as their negative and if we can focus on the good side that is what we will get more of. Set this way of thinking as an example in your classroom and your children will do it too – it's catching!

The above reframes are mostly how to reframe yourself. You see a seemingly awful, uncomfortable situation and you literally change the internal focus, take it differently and therefore can respond differently. This may take a little practice. It certainly helps if your fellow teachers know what you are up to, as discussions about how 'bad', 'wrong' or 'terrible' kids are will not help the process of reframing!

When using reframing with children, it is important to consider their cognitive level. We understand children who are 7 years old or younger overgeneralize how they see their strengths and weaknesses (Piaget and Inhelder 1969). It may not be effective then, for an adult to speak about only one aspect of what the child does as a problem. The child may not have the cognitive capacity to understand that difference and, therefore, a reframing will not be possible. For example, a teacher trying to reframe the fighting of two 5 year olds as a sign of trying to connect with each another may find that the attempt falls on deaf ears!

If you are in the process of using reframing on others and not just internally, it's important to know that young children may not be able to follow a reframe cognitively but they may be able to follow a shift related to emotions. For example, a child sensitive to non-verbal changes in the emotional climate, such as making a joke and laughing about a situation absurdly, will be able to benefit from this emotional and non-verbal shaking of the boundaries or reframing. This type of reframing is at an experiential level (or let's say non-linear, non-logical type) as opposed to a cognitive one. When you watch some comedians, you can notice that they operate at this level to great effect.

How many reframes have you presented today? What were they?

Concluding thoughts

When presenting a reframe to another person:

- Make sure you have rapport and their permission to offer it.
- You may believe your reframe is the best ever and yet it may not work for the other person – simply because they have a different model of the world than you do. Remember the NLP presupposition from Chapter 1 'There is no such thing as failure, only feedback', and explore other possible reframes.
- If you present the reframe in the form of a question or a metaphor, it will most likely be more fully considered by your subject than if you present it as a statement of fact.
- I find too many NLP novices saying they 'reframed' someone, when in fact you cannot reframe anyone other than yourself. The best you can do is to ask someone to consider your reframe and then they can choose whether or not it reframes their own experience.

Journal ideas to look into

If you want to practise reframing, start by viewing all situations you come across from different perspectives. Take an opposing point of view to that you may normally have and see the way you can fully cross any borders to find new ways of experiencing viewpoints.

- How do companies compile dictionaries?
- What attributes meaning to words?
- What needs to be in place to really make a reframe work?

Metaphors

Some years ago while running a class for Swedish students delivering information about metaphors, I was asked by a student, 'what exactly is a metaphor?' I answered that it was just like a story but has very influential pieces to it. 'Why don't you just call it a story then?' was the retort I got back. After consideration, I decided not to answer her question directly, or challenge the challenge, so I told her this: 'Just imagine, in times before newspapers, television, the internet or any kind of expanded communication systems, other ways had to be evolved to allow people to know what's going on in the world. When you tune in to the way they did this, it was in the form of a poem, plays and songs. Inside these forms was all the information you may need.'

We are all very familiar with the use of metaphor, we all know that a metaphor is the use of words or phrases to directly compare a seemingly unrelated thing, the Compact Oxford English dictionary defines it thus: a figure of speech in which a word or phrase is applied to something to which it is not literally applicable (e.g. *food for thought*) or a thing symbolic of something else. The term metaphor originally comes from Greek metaphora (meta, meaning 'over', and herein, 'to carry'). This transfer (or carry) of meaning is found in all cultures and languages, and has a long history of use as evidenced in the teaching of Aristotle and Plato.

Lakoff and Johnson (1980) have this to say about metaphor:

> In all aspects of life ... we define our reality in terms of metaphors and then proceed to act on the basis of the metaphors. We draw inferences, set goals, make commitments, and execute plans, all on the basis of how we in part structure our experience, consciously and unconsciously, by means of metaphor. (p. 158)

Parables and allegories use language metaphorically, and again here you can see how great communicators of the past have used metaphor to excellent effect – Jesus Christ, Ghandi, Socrates, Descartes and more modern examples are Winston Churchill, J F Kennedy, Nelson Mandela. A simple leap then can take us into the classroom (notice the metaphor?) and we see how useful metaphor can be. In teaching we use metaphor through story, poetry, art all of the time, but are we sufficiently aware about what we are doing? In this part of the chapter we try to encourage you to raise that awareness so that you can switch into metaphor mode more easily and illustrate how metaphor can be used in the classroom to enhance achievement.

Metaphor works on the conscious and deep mind simultaneously, the conscious mind being concerned with the details of the story or 'face value', while the deep mind will process the symbolic meanings and make the learning transferable to other situations. We can embed messages into a story that the listener is barely aware of – politicians and advertisers are doing this all of the time.

We all have our own story and we change this story as we travel through life. The story may well seem unrecognizable to someone who knows us well but it is, none the less, a metaphor of our life – but it is not our life; remember, the map is not the territory. In the same way, the life story is not the life. We can change the way we see our lives through the story we write about it and in this way change the way we live, hopefully for the better.

In education we learn and have learnt a lot about learning styles and about how we need to teach to the style of the individual student. Your understanding of NLP so far will have reinforced that view, and that we have to calibrate on behaviour and learn what individuals need in their effective communication. There are lots of tests you can do to ascertain learning style but many I have seen seem to be both time consuming and pigeon-holing and therefore one is not really calibrating on the individual but putting the person into a box. It's a bit like reading your horoscope; you know that it covers a whole band of people all born at different times in the month and different years and yet there is a paragraph in the newspaper every day that is meant to address one twelfth of the population. The more you think about this, the less sense it makes, but maybe there is a grain of truth in it. (Notice the metaphors again?) Wouldn't it be better to be able to carry the skills internally with you for assessing learning styles. Well you can! Intuitively you have all the skills you need to ascertain learning styles, and with a bit of fine-tuning you can switch these skills on and teach in the right style. By listening to the metaphors as well as other aspects of children's language you can ascertain modalities more effectively.

Judging from personal experience, metaphors are the most powerful ways of getting information across that I have found. Different uses of metaphor reflect people's sociocultural constructions of the world and can indicate what is significant in a particular culture and what is personally significant to those who create metaphors. Many have argued that metaphors make us, rather than us making metaphors (Stacey 1997), and this influence may have more significance than we realize for children's development.

Think back to the special stories that have influenced you in your life and consider why they had such influence. What happened inside you when you heard, and again 'hear' these metaphors?

If you were to shadow one of your classes through a school day, you'd probably be exposed to a wide range of teaching techniques. Some aspects of our colleagues' teaching can really make a difference to our own lessons. Outlined below are some different techniques that can really help to motivate pupils and get them to approach your subject from an unexpected angle.

Using metaphors

Figurative language, for instance, doesn't just belong in the English lesson. Metaphors, in particular, can be effective and powerful learning tools when used in other subjects. They can:

- link abstracts to concrete language
- open the mind to multiple levels of understanding
- promote and encourage emotions
- aid memory for all students by creating associations or links (this is especially effective for learners with Specific Learning Difficulties and, in particular, those with short-term memory issues)
- facilitate unspoken or unconscious learning
- help learners to make sense of information and issues
- assist in gaining understanding about the ways your learners 'see things'.

You can use them as a device to springboard discussion: metaphors allow pupils to explore their feelings in a safe, non-judgemental way and to clarify these emotions by using revealing images or comparisons.

Metaphors in the classroom – finding out about children's learning using metaphor

Metaphors are wonderful indicators of the sense a person favours. To begin with, you can ask a person to give you an indication, through metaphor, of their internal experience.

Ask them something like this:

'When you're learning, what is that learning like?'

You are looking for sensory data. Here's an example of what you are encouraging.

Learning is...

Wading through mud

Eating something really hard to chew that stays in your mouth for ages and then you don't know how to get rid of it

Painting a picture

A long, long journey I will be on for a long time

Being in the dark for ages then a light comes on and I can work it out

Whatever answer comes, encourage further development with:

'And is there anything else about that learning?' 'What's it really like?'

You can see that people's metaphors on the experience of learning differ and they will differ according to the situation you are in and what you are learning.

Ask yourself, when I am learning, what is learning like...?

Children writing with metaphors

Fraser (2006) describes how she used metaphor to facilitate learning by impressing a 'concept or idea through the powerful image or vividness of the expression. In addition, metaphor can capture the inexpressible in that what a metaphor conveys is virtually impossible to express in any other way without losing the potency of the message.'

Metaphors require the brain to do a little gymnastics to be able to understand the meaning the speaker is trying to convey and, sometimes, when the metaphor is understood, the meaning will be far deeper than if simple literal language were used. This is why poetry can be so meaningful and evocative in so few words.

Fraser achieved excellent results in the area when she took a cohort of volunteer children and explored dimensions of humanity, inspired by the work of Gendler (1988), from pleasure to pain. Gendler writes about these human emotions and experiences as if they were real people. For example, 'Worry has written the definitive work on nervous habits'. 'She etches lines on people's foreheads when they are not paying attention' and 'Sensuality does not wear a watch but she always gets to the essential places on time'.

Using Gendler's descriptions as a stimulus the children discussed qualities of their teacher as if that quality were a person they might meet. The children were then encouraged to select a quality or emotion of their own choosing to write about. In each class the children showed much enthusiasm for writing in this manner. So for example 'Hope and Madness' were chosen and you can see the results below.

Poems reprinted with the kind permission of Debora Fraser. For further poems, see Appendix 1.

Hope

She wears a pale white cloak
Her eyes are blue and seem to glow
Her face is lit up as though she has been waiting for something
For a long time and finally it has come.
Her hair is raven black and in it she wears a pearl white ribbon.
Wherever she walks, good things happen as if to make a trail.
Her best friend is Joy because to be hopeful you must have first experienced Joy.
She has had many jobs like a nurse and a biologist for both jobs involve helping.
She understands people and is never greedy.
She is fair and is a gainer and a giver.
She has what is important, that is friends.
If you are ever to meet her, remember that first impressions do not matter to her.

(Kate F., age 10)

Madness

He wears a bright red silk coat
And lives in a world of anger.
He eats chillies and wasabi
And drinks wasabi water.
His job is a rates collector.
His nature is fire.
He wants to kill Happiness.
Watch out, he is slinky.

(Richard, age 8)

Communicating from the inner world of the child

As you can see, the metaphorical writing shows a depth of understanding that otherwise might not be expressed. Other quicker ways of getting into the metaphor groove can be done by 5 or 10 minute exercises at the beginning of sessions with a round of 'If I were an animal I would be a...', 'If I were a car I would be a...', 'If I were a colour I would be a...'. Try this for yourself right now.

If I were an animal I would be a...
If I were a car I would be a...
If I were a colour I would be a...
If I were the weather I would be...

Now think of some other things you could associate with...

Using a narrative approach to overcome behaviour problems

Using metaphor encourages the externalization of thoughts and feelings. In my work with students with ADHD, one of the techniques I have used is to encourage the child to give their behaviour a name. So, working with Mikel, he called his ADHD behaviour 'the Abdabs'; he was then able to distinguish between himself – Mikel – as a person, and the behaviour as the Abdabs. Once this distinction existed, it was possible for the Mikel to engage in a challenge to see how much of each day have 'the Abdabs' been in control and how much of the day has Mikel been in control. This technique can be used with many other emotions like anger, anxiety, shyness, and so on. You may like to try this one yourself; maybe you are on a diet at the moment and you could think about how much of the day 'the Munchies' are in control and how much you are.

My name for the behaviour I want to get control over
Proportion of the day I have been in control   %
Proportion of the day the unwanted behaviour has been in control   %
Saying for tomorrow 'Today I gain a little more control'.

Multi-sensory imagination

Don't forget to use lots of multi-sensory language when providing activities for your learners. Consider what sort of language you are using to evoke a response. Remember, we all have slightly differing styles of learning. To evoke a multi-sensory response, ask multi-sensory questions:

Kinaesthetic imagination: 'Imagine how that would feel? How might you act on this?'

Visualization: 'Can you imagine what that would look like?'

Auditory imagination: 'Imagine you can hear the story and it's details ... what would it sound like?'

Make a note of the number of times you consciously used multi-sensory language in your classroom today.

What subject areas were they in?

Can you extend this use to other areas?

Case study: the use of metaphor

You never know how much difference a metaphor can make in someone's life!

I was asked to talk to a 6 year old girl, Megan, by her mother. Megan had contracted asthma three years previously and her mother knew how I used metaphor to hear and speak effectively with kids and adults. I used a toy to talk through with her to find out about whatever was happening in Megan's life and it went well. She could talk much more freely when she was talking through a rabbit and the rabbit knew things that Megan didn't, even if the rabbit was herself!

After this 'talk' that we had, she seemed satisfied with what we had discovered about some undisclosed 'truths' in her life, but then turned to me and asked me a question that rooted me to the spot. She put her head in her hands and said to me, 'I just wish I knew more about what life is all about…'

Just imagine the responsibility I felt at that time. I stood there, with a thousand thoughts whirring around amuck inside my mind. I looked through the window to let providence guide me. As I saw the flowers and plants waving gently in the wind, something came to me that would let us both feel more relieved. 'See that plant outside, Megan', I said. 'Yes', she replied curiously. 'Well, if you were to watch that plant grow, it would start from just a stem and growing leaves as it gets older. It doesn't know what flower it will be all at once, but all the information for the plant is in the seed, so the plant will always know what to do, but only one leaf at a time.' She was extremely pleased with this metaphor and quickly got back into her life once more, not encumbered by her past issues.

Before that particular day, Megan had had asthma every year, for the previous three years. To this day, her asthma has never come back, as far as I know!

So, am I saying that metaphor cures illnesses? Well, no and yes: yet there is evident proof that metaphors get messages across effectively and deeply.

The following is another metaphor that struck me as perfect for teaching or training. I was returning from school one day and a runaway horse, with a bridle on, sped past a group of us into a farmer's yard, evidently seeking water to drink. The horse was perspiring heavily. The farmer didn't recognize it so we cornered it and I hopped onto the horse's back. Since it had a bridle on, I took hold of the reins, cried 'Giddy-up' and headed for the road. I was confident the horse would turn in the right direction, yet I didn't know what that direction was. The horse trotted and at times galloped along. Now and then he would forget he was on the highway and start to go into a field. So I would pull on the bit and call his attention to the fact the highway was where he was supposed to be. Finally, about four miles from where I had mounted him, he turned into a farmyard and the farmer said, 'So the runaway has come back. Where did you find him?' I replied, 'About four miles from here.' 'How did you know you should come here?' I explained, 'I didn't know. The horse knew. All I did was keep his attention on the road.' This metaphor has several different slants, yet you can see its value in defining a teacher/pupil relationship.

One of my favourite metaphors talks about commitment. There was a time when for boys as well as men the cap one wore was a lifetime treasure. Then, perhaps when running across fields, boys came across a wall or obstacle that they couldn't climb easily, they'd throw their caps over the obstacle. That way they knew they would make sure they'd *have* to climb it!

'So what is a metaphor?', I was asked back in Sweden. And why didn't I just call them stories? Perhaps you can now see for yourselves that a metaphor can carry the narrative, emotion, pictures, sounds, feelings and thinking that connect with the inner minds of each speaker and listener. You could say that a metaphor will 'carry' a story. Personally, I like to read many metaphors, learn a few and see the way they are put together, then let myself start constructing them, trusting the deeper part of my brain to bring the plan together.

> Think of a time in the past when you used metaphor to good effect with another person, it could be at home or at work...

How to design metaphors

For those of you who like process and structure, here's a method of designing metaphors.

The major purpose of a metaphor is to pace and lead a client's behaviour through a story. The major points of construction consist of:

1. Displacing the referential index from the client to a character in a story.
2. Pacing the person's problem by establishing behaviours and events between the characters in the story that are similar to those in the person's situation.
3. Accessing resources for the person within the context of the story.
4. Finishing the story such that a sequence of events occurs in which the characters in the story resolve the conflict and achieve the desired outcome.

Generating a metaphor – basic steps

The basic steps to generate a metaphor are as follows.

Premapping

1. *Identify the sequence of behaviour and/or events in question.* This could range from a conflict between beliefs, to a physical illness, to problematic interrelationships between the individual client and parents, a boss or a spouse, pupil and teachers.

2. *Strategy analysis.* Is there any consistent sequence of representations contributing to the current behavioural outcome?

3. *Identify the desired new outcomes and choices.* This may be done at any level of detail, and it is important that you have an outcome to work for.

4. *Establish anchors for strategic elements* involved in this current behaviour and the desired outcome. For instance, in one knee you might anchor all of the strategies and representations that stop the person from having the necessary choices; on the other knee you might anchor any personal resources (regardless of specific contexts) that the person may have.

Mapping strategies

5. *Displace referential indices.* Map over all nouns (objects and elements) to establish the characters in the story. The characters may be anything, animate or inanimate, from rocks to forest creatures to cowboys to books, etc. What you choose as characters is not important so long as you preserve the character relationship. Very often you may want to use characters from well-known fairy tales and myths.

6. *Establish an isomorphism between the person's situation and behaviour, and the situation and behaviours of the characters in the story – map over all verbs* (relations and interactions). Assign behavioural traits, such as strategies and representational characteristics, that parallel those in the client's present situation (i.e. pace the person's situation with the story). Make use of any anchors you have established previously to secure the relationship.

7. *Access and establish new resources in terms of the characters and events in the story.* This may be done within the framework of a reframing or reaccessing of a forgotten resource; again, using any appropriate pre-established anchors. You may choose to keep the actual content of the resource ambiguous, allowing the person's unconscious processes to choose the appropriate one.

8. *Use non sequiturs, ambiguities and direct quotes* to break up sequences in the story and direct conscious resistance, if such resistance is present and is hindering the effect of the metaphor. Conscious understanding does not, of course, necessarily interfere with the metaphoric process.

9. *Keep your resolution as ambiguous as necessary* to allow the person's unconscious processes to make the appropriate changes. Collapse the *pre-established anchors* and role-play the new scenario into the future, if possible, to *check your work.*

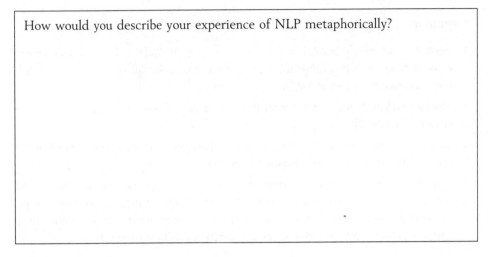

How would you describe your experience of NLP metaphorically?

Summary

Metaphors have educational uses beyond the cognitive and literary. They can provide poignant insights and enhance emotional development. Children have the capacity to create metaphors that reveal personal values, emotional and spiritual awareness that can belie their chronological age. Personifying emotions is one way that children can employ metaphors that explore the inner landscapes of their lives.

Conclusion

You have now been introduced to the NLP view of Anchoring, Reframing and Metaphor. Take some time to write your reflections in your journal. You may feel that none of this is new to you, or you may feel that it puts a new spin on things you already use in slightly differing ways. You will have views though and it's a good thing to write them down and allow your deep mind to bring things to the surface. Think about opportunities to use the techniques, consider getting some practical training to help you sharpen up your existing skills and become a more excellent communicator. The quiz overleaf will help to embed learning.

Chapter 4 quiz

	True	False	Maybe
1. Anchors should only be used on others in the classroom			
2. Anchoring happens when a state is so strongly associated with a stimulus that the object or event is associated with that state from then on			
3. Positive and negative anchors are just as easy to set up			
4. Anchors need to be only visual to be really useful			
5. Old negative experiences can be collapsed using anchors			
6. Motivation to get a task done more easily can be overcome by setting anchors			
7. You cannot take powerful states that are inside you and move them to any object, time or place			
8. You can get into states and transfer them to others so they can experience it for themselves; you can do this via metaphors, anecdotes or your passion for using language skilfully			
9. The more you bring up powerful states and place them on objects or yourself (for instance, a knuckle, knee or table top), the more these states can build and multiply the strength			
10. If you, or a pupil, are not in a good state, you can access your/their own internal anchors by asking what you/they love in life and when you see them inside that state, you can introduce the negative state and it should disappear			
11. Your classroom and home are full of anchors, you can make these even more effective by setting them consciously			
12. Any situation or event can be reframed more positively or negatively			
13. Presenting your reframe as a metaphor or question will engage the listener better than a bold statement			
14. Reframing has to be verbal			
15. The words we use to communicate, whether it be through speech, sign or writing, are interpretations devised by humans for the purpose of conveying meaning			

16. Metaphor is good for both introducing and reviewing sessions			
17. Using metaphor well in the classroom is hard to do and requires years of practice			
18. You need to have built up excellent rapport with your class before you start using metaphor			
19. Metaphor is one of the most powerful tools in a teacher's tool kit			

Answers and discussion can be found on page 143.

5 Meta and Milton Models of hypnotic language

History

The Meta Model, NLP's first formal model, was published in 1975 by Richard Bandler and John Grinder in their ground-breaking book *The Structure of Magic, Volume 1*. It extended features of general semantics (Korzybski) and transformational grammar (Chomsky).

The basic principle behind the Meta Model is Alfred Korzybski's (1931) notion that 'the map is not the territory'. That is, the models we make of the world around us using our brains and our language are not the world itself but representations of it. We literally have whole worlds built of linguistics in our minds which are not the whole truth but act as if they are. You know how it goes. Kerry says 'I can't do that.' You know she can. So you tell her, and then you both find yourselves in an argument in which her self-limiting belief is strengthened by your well-intentioned comments.

The Meta Model in Neuro-Linguistic Programming is a set of skilful questions designed to specify information that challenges and expands the limits of a person's model of the world. It responds to the distortions, generalizations, and deletions in the speaker's language. The Meta Model forms the basis of Neuro-Linguistic Programming as developed by then assistant professors of linguistics John Grinder and Richard Bandler. Grinder and Bandler explained how people create faulty mental maps of reality in language, failing to test their linguistic/cognitive models against the experience of their senses.

The diagram shown in Figure 6 illustrates that what your filter systems claim to be reality are simply more 'maps of the territories' and not real at all. In other words, what you perceive is, in fact, a *projection* derived from information passing through the filter systems.

What We Perceive We Create

Figure 7

Deletion, distortion and generalization

As described by Bandler and Grinder, **deletion** is a process by which we selectively pay attention to certain dimensions of our experience and exclude others. Take, for example, the ability that people have to filter out or exclude all other sounds in a room full of people talking in order to listen to one particular person's voice. Deletion reduces the world to proportions which we feel capable of handling. The reduction may be useful in some contexts and yet be the source of pain in others.

Distortion is the process which allows us to make shifts in our experience of sensory data. Fantasy, for example, allows us to prepare for experiences which we may have before they occur. It is the process which has made possible all the artistic creations which we as humans have produced. Similarly, all the great novels, all the revolutionary discoveries of the sciences, involve the ability to distort and mis-represent present reality.

Generalization is the process by which elements or pieces of a person's model become detached from their original experience and come to represent the entire category, of which the experience is an example. Our ability to generalize is essential to coping with the world. The same process of generalization may lead a human being to establish a rule such as, 'I don't express my feelings'.

The function, then, of the Meta Model is to help us identify lost language in the 'reality' of life as others are trying to express it, and to use the Meta Model to recover the lost linguistics.

Definition

People respond to events based on their internal pictures, sounds and feelings. They also collect these experiences into groups or categories that are labelled with words. The Meta Model is a method for helping someone get from the 'poor' internal word maps back to the specific sensory-based experiences they are based on. It is here in the information-rich specific experiences that useful changes can be made that will result in changes in behaviour.

What follows is a description of the different types of 'sloppy thinking' and examples of such. You will find a table on pages 100–1 that summarizes the Meta Model.

The Meta Model language patterns (much of this was based on the work of family therapist Virginia Satir, gestalt therapist Fritz Perls and linguistic patterns from transformational syntax) yield a fuller representation of the client's model of the world. We can get to the deep structure (or truth of the person's world) by offering challenges to its (the person's view) limits, by means of sifting through the distortions, generalizations or deletions in the speaker's language.

The language we use can delete, distort and generalize the totality we call our worlds – thinking and communication. When you recognize that a person has a kind of speaking (and listening) that gets in the way of their success or happiness it is very tempting to want to tell them the error of their ways. After all, once you point out to them how ineffective they are being, then they are sure to thank you and change their ways, right?

Obviously not! None of us like being told that we are wrong and that the speaker is right. So we energetically defend our beliefs, even the daft ones. In fact, the strength with which we adhere to our position and points of view reflects the degree to which we feel we have to defend them!

The more you argue with a person and tell them how wrong they are, the more you strengthen the language patterns that you wish to loosen.

What to do? Use two tools: questions and the Meta Model. Add in huge amounts of rapport, good observational skills and the ability to be quiet while the other person thinks things through. Patience is also important (because strong self-limiting beliefs respond best to a very gradual softly, softly approach, rather than a full frontal attack backed by the force of your personality).

Throughout this chapter there are the usual spaces for you to add in your own thinking and examples – do this as you go along because it will really help you in your grasp of this very important area.

How to use the Meta Model

The following will get you thinking.

Let's say, for example, that Jack says *'I can tell I won't do well in this subject by the looks the teacher gives me! That makes me sad because I never have any luck with teachers.'*

At first glance these are fairly understandable comments, yet when we apply the Meta Model to them we learn a little more, as demonstrated below:

(a) Jack believes he can read the teacher's mind. This is an erroneous belief unless he is a very gifted clairvoyant!

(b) He also believes that the appearance of her facial muscles enables him to predict what her likely response will be (check back on the mind-reading errors from sensory awareness). In reality, he is looking at her expression and deciding things from his own 'map of the territory' and not from purely sensory awareness.

(c) He has a very limiting belief that he never has any 'luck with teachers'. This is a generalization – a belief which rests on skimpy and carefully selected evidence. While it is possible that it is true, it is rather unlikely; what is more likely is that he is using the memory of a number of setbacks to generalize the past, so as to predict that the future will simply be more of the same – and to trap himself in a prison of his own debilitating beliefs.

(d) In saying that 'this makes me sad' Jack is announcing that he believes that his emotions are the result of outside events over which he has no control. But the way in which he announces this ensures that he remains a victim – since his comment implies no ownership of the difficulty! He 'is' a victim, but a victim of his own thinking rather than of events.

To assist Jack we could use the Meta Model to alert him to how his predicament results from his own less-than-useful thinking. And, rather than lecture him on the error of his ways, we can do this in the most subtle manner – by simply asking a seemingly innocuous question or two. We'll come on to these shortly!

We have distinguished a finite amount of 'sloppy thinking' patterns and how to challenge them. There is a table on pages 100–1 to assist you in learning these.

Firstly, you'll need some of these distinctions in your own mind. We'll start with *distortions* (remember that our sloppy thinking has derived from distortions, generalizations and deletions of the whole truth).

Distortions

Presupposition (a type of distortion when used in a sloppy way). The presupposition refers to an assumption whereby the truth is taken for granted.

Crucially, negation of an expression does not change its presupposition: *I want to do it again* and *I don't want to do it again* both mean that the subject has done it *already* one or more times; *My school is good* and *my school is not good* both mean that the subject has a school to go to. In this respect, the presupposition is distinguished from entailment and implication. For example, *the president was assassinated* entails that the president is dead, but if the expression is negated, the entailment is not necessarily true.

Example 1:

- 'My teacher is terrible.'
- Presupposition: You have a teacher.
- Challenge: 'How exactly is he/she terrible?' (recovers lost information).

Example 2:

- 'Do you want me to do it again?'
- Presupposition: I have done it already, at least once.
- Challenge: 'Have you done it before, properly yet?'

Example 3:

- 'My mum is as lazy as me, that's why I can't do it.'
- Presuppositions: You have a mother; you say she's lazy.
- Challenge: 'Am I to assume that you are wanting the same bad habits?' (at least you will get more information about the motivation of the pupil).

Have a go at drafting your own example:

Cause–effect

Cause–effect, the inappropriate use of causal thinking (x means y, x makes me y, or x makes y happen) is considered semantically ill-formed and unacceptable.

Causality always implies at least some relationship of dependency between the cause and the effect. For example, deeming something a cause may imply that, all other things being equal, if the cause occurs the effect does as well, or at least that the probability of the effect occurring increases.

Example 1:

- 'That comment makes me angry.'
- Challenge: 'If it weren't for that comment, you would not be angry?'

Example 2:

- 'Being late means I can't catch up.'
- Challenge: 'How, specifically, does you being late mean you are choosing not to catch up?'

> Have a go at drafting your own example:
>
>
>
>
>
>
>
>

Mind read

Mind-reading violation occurs when someone claims to think they know what another is thinking without verification.

Example:

- Jack says *'I can tell I won't do well in this subject by the looks the teacher gives me!' 'That makes me sad because I never have any luck with teachers.'*
- Challenge: 'How do you know that look from the teacher means you won't do well?'
- 'You don't like me.'
- 'Have I told you I don't like you?' 'What would happen if I did/didn't?'

> Have a go at drafting your own example:
>
>
>
>
>

Nominalization

Nominalization occurs when a verb is transformed into a noun. A dynamic process (i.e. a verb) is transformed into something static (i.e. a noun). It's like taking a snapshot of a moving object, you don't see the movement any more, just the (static) object.

What we are looking to do is retrieve lost information and look at the process the person is experiencing, rather than the 'labels' that are apparent.

Examples:

- 'The _communication_ in this school is poor.'
- Challenge: 'How could we communicate more effectively?' 'Who is not communicating with whom?'

- 'They need my _decision_ by Monday.'
- Challenge: 'What are you deciding?' 'What decision?'

Note: there are two simple tests that can be used to determine if a word or expression is a nominalization:

- The wheelbarrow test: if you can put it into a wheelbarrow, it is NOT a nominalization (e.g. a drink is a type of noun, but it is not a nominalization ... it is tangible, it can be put into a wheelbarrow and carried around. The phrase _Quality Control_ fails the wheelbarrow test and is a nominalization.

Have a go at drafting your own example:

Complex equivalence

Complex equivalence draws an unrelated conclusion from an event to create some supposed logic that, when scrutinized, does not follow. Complex equivalence puts two things together that may have no business being together, but can sound plausible.

Examples:

- 'And now the head has left, I'll have twice as much work by the end of the year!'
- Challenge: 'Are you telling me your out-tray depended entirely on your head?'

- 'The results mean that I am not succeeding at all.'
- Challenge: 'Do you always judge yourself on results and not on what ongoing progress you can see from being here?'
- Another challenge: 'You're not succeeding in the way you're looking at it.' 'How would you like to succeed in the future?'

Have a go at drafting your own example:

Generalizations

Universals

Universals are words that want to encompass a great audience just as a result of their utterance. Many people who seek to use one-upmanship will use universals in an effort to gain authority for their cause.

For example:

- '*Every* time I ask you a question, you grimace.'
- '*Everyone* in the waiting room had at least one complaint against Dr Parker.'
- 'There's *always* somebody in his class that will not pass.'
- '*All* educated people are intelligent.'

Universal quantifiers occur when someone attempts to characterize something as true for everything, everyone or all those in a set. In these NLP Meta Models questions can be used when someone is generalizing too broadly.

Example:

- 'My pupils are all lazy.'
- Challenge: 'All of them?' or 'Which pupils, specifically?'

Modal operators

Modal operators are intuitively characterized by expressing a modal attitude, such as necessity (have to, must, should) or possibility (can, might, may) towards the proposition which it is applied to.

Example:

- 'I can't pull myself together.'
- Challenge: 'What would happen if you did/didn't?'

> Have a go at drafting your own example:

Deletions

Simple deletions

In a simple deletion an important element in a statement is missing. For example:

- Go and do it. That is important. I feel bad.
- Keywords to look out for are *it* and *that*.

The appropriate response would be to ask what, where or when exactly?

- 'Go and do what exactly?'

> Have a go at drafting your own example:

Unspecified verbs

In an unspecified verb it is not clear how the action creates or created the result. For example:

- 'I created a poor impression on them.'

The appropriate response is to ask how exactly does taking 'x' action lead to 'y' result. 'How exactly did you create a poor impression on whom exactly?'

> Have a go at drafting your own example:

Comparative deletions

Comparative deletions are a comparative in which the starting point for comparison is not stated, which is also the deletion. These comparisons are frequently found in advertising. For example, in typical assertions such as 'our chickens have more flavour', 'our TV pictures are sharper' or '50% more', there is no mention of what it is they are comparing a thing to. In some cases it is easy to infer what the missing element in a comparative is. In other cases the speaker or writer may have been deliberately vague in this regard, for example 'Glasgow's miles better'.

So, for example, if someone states that they are 'too fat', they must be comparing without letting us know who with (which is the deleted part). In China in older times, it was good to be 'fatter' as it showed abundance and affluence!

Examples:

- 'I'm too fat.'
- Challenge: 'Compared to who?' (gets you the lost information)

- 'That wasn't the best plan.'
- Challenge: 'What were some of the other plans?'

- 'I am a bad learner.'
- Challenge: 'Bad, compared to whom?'

> Have a go at drafting your own example:

Lack of referential index

Unspecified referential index, refers to the use of a personal pronoun when the context is unknown, or cannot easily be understood based on the preceding sentences. For example, uncontextualized use of they, them, you.

Examples:

- 'They say I should do my A-levels, but I don't know if I have the confidence.'
- Challenge: 'Who is it that says you should do your A-levels?' 'What do you mean by confidence?'

- 'Yeah, people have tried mind-mapping before and it doesn't work for you.'
- Challenge: 'Wait, what people/who exactly?'

- 'I hate watching England play. We always lose and it makes me depressed.'
- Challenge: 'By "we", do you mean that you are part of the England team?'

- 'Research has shown us that it's true.'
- Challenge: 'What research exactly?' 'Who was it that made the research and what were they looking for?'

Have a go at drafting your own example:

Lost performative

Lost performative makes reference to an action but the person who performed the action is unspecified.

Examples:

- 'Her book was highly acclaimed.'
- Challenge: 'Highly acclaimed by whom?' or 'How do you know that?'

- 'The lesson was judged as highly successful.'
- Challenge: 'Judged by whom?'

So as you can see that the Meta Model is a highly sophisticated set of linguistic tools to recover the lost 'world' of information in disabling situations. Once you have recovered the information from the speaker, you'll find the problem disappears. Either that or they will look at you very strangely and walk off and try to lay the story on someone else!

So how will you use this model in class? Perhaps you'll find it useful in meetings with parents, even your fellow teachers?

Have a go at drafting your own example:

How to use the Meta Model

The following are some pointers:

1. Take one category at a time and practise it for a week or two (see the list overleaf).

2. Listen for the Meta Model violation (where the speaker's language deletes, distorts or generalizes a portion of the whole story) only during the first couple of minutes of the conversation – otherwise you are unlikely to take a very active role on the conversation!

3. The Meta Model 'challenges' or coaching questions need to be used with great caution. Use the challenges when you have very good rapport and calibration (ways to determine what you see in front of you specifically) skills.

4. Be careful to avoid overusing the coaching questions – otherwise the Meta Model can become an interrogation tool. The section on rapport (see Chapter 2) should hold you in good stead while asking quite intrusive questions.

Here's a way to learn it:

We have given you the table overleaf, so you can copy it and learn some of the patterns. If you just look at the patterns and learn a few, you'll find them popping out of your mouth when appropriate.

The Meta Model chart

DISTORTIONS		
1. Mind Reading: Claiming to know someone's internal state. Ex: 'You don't like me.'	'How do you know I don't like you?'	Recovers source of the information.
2. Lost Performative: Value judgements where the person doing the judging is left out. Ex. 'It's bad to be inconsistent.'	'Who says it's bad?' 'According to whom?' 'How do you know it's bad.'	Gathers evidence. Recovers source of the belief, the Performative, strategy for the belief.
3. Cause–effect: Where cause is wrongly put outside the self. Ex: 'You make me sad.'	'How does what I'm doing cause you to choose to feel sad?' (Also, Counter Ex., or 'How specifically?'	Recovers the choice.
4. Complex Equivalence: Where two experiences are interpreted as being synonymous. Ex: 'She's always yelling at me, she doesn't like me.'	'How does her yelling mean that she...' 'Have you ever yelled at someone you liked?'	Recovers Complex Equivalence. Counter Example.
5. Presuppositions: Ex: 'If my husband knew how much I suffered, he wouldn't do that.' There are three presuppositions in this sentence: (1) I suffer, (2) My husband acts in some way, and (3) My husband doesn't know I suffer.	(1) 'How do you choose to suffer?' (2) 'How is he (re)acting?' (3) 'How do you know he doesn't know?'	Specify the choice and the verb, and and what he does. Recover the Internal Rep., and the Complex Equivalence.
GENERALIZATIONS		
6. Universal Quantifiers: Universal Generalizations such as all, every, never, everyone, no one, etc. Ex: 'She never listens to me.'	Find Counter Examples. 'Never?' 'What would happen if she did?'	Recovers Counter Examples, Effects, Outcomes.
7. Modal Operators: a. Modal Operators of Necessity: As in should, shouldn't, must, must not, have to, need to, it is necessary. Ex: 'I have to take care of her.'	a. 'What would happen if you did?' ('What would happen if you didn't?' Also,'Or?'	Recovers Effects, Outcome.
b. Modal Operators of Possibility: (Or Impossibility.) As in can/can't, will/won't, may/may not, possible/impossible. Ex: 'I can't tell him the truth.'	b. 'What prevents you?' ('What would happen if you did?')	Recovers Causes.

DELETIONS		
8. Nominalizations: Process words which have been frozen in time, making them nouns. Ex: 'There is no communication here.'	"'Who's not communicating what to whom?' 'How would you like to communicate?'	Turns it back into a process, recovers deletion, and Ref. Index.
9. Unspecified Verbs: Ex: 'He rejected me.'	'How, specifically?'	Specifies the verb.
10. Simple Deletions: a. Simple Deletions: Ex: 'I am uncomfortable.'	a. 'About what/ whom?'	Recovers Deletion.
b. Lack of Referential Index: Fails to specify a person or thing. Ex: 'They don't listen to me.'	b. 'Who, specifically, doesn't listen to you?'	Recovers Ref. Index.
c. Comparative Deletions: As in good, better, best, worst, more, less, most, least. Ex: 'She's a better person.'	c. 'Better than whom?' 'Better at what?' 'Compared to whom, what?'	Recovers Comparative Deletion.

Questions for your journal:

1. Now you have read this piece, what does the Meta Model mean to you?

2. What are the three big distinctions the Meta Model is built on?

3. If a pupil came to you and said 'you don't like me', how would you respond using the Meta Model and which category of Meta Model violation is it?

Milton Model

The Milton Model lists the key parts of speech and key patterns that are useful in directing another person's line of thinking by being 'artfully vague', and in principle the Milton Model states that larger chunks (more general use of language) can lead to more rapport, while smaller chunks (more specific language) are more limiting and have a greater chance of excluding concepts from a person's experience.

In relation to the mind, I've used the words deep mind to describe the working of the subconscious mind and dominant to describe the working of the conscious mind.

The patterns of the Milton Model can be used to

- pace another person's reality to gain rapport

- access deep mind resources of another person to gather information or to lead them into an altered state

- distract the conscious or dominant mind if it's too busy.

Indirect methods

Milton Erickson was generally regarded as the foremost language master of his time. He worked with linguistics from 1930 to 1980 and used cleverly structured sentences full of vague meanings to help his clients discover how to address their problems and the resources that they already had available to them.

Erickson maintained that it was not possible to consciously instruct the deep mind, and that authoritarian suggestions were likely to be met with resistance (well, that's no secret to you in the classroom is it!). The sub-dominant mind responds to openings, opportunities, metaphors and contradictions. Effective suggestion, then, should be 'artfully vague', leaving space for the subject to fill in the gaps with their own sub-dominant understandings – even if they do not consciously grasp what is happening. The skilled teacher constructs these gaps of meaning in a way most suited to the individual subject – in a way which is most likely to produce the desired change.

The Milton Model is purposely vague and metaphoric and is used to soften the Meta Model and make indirect suggestions. A direct suggestion merely states the goal. For example, 'When you are in front of the audience you will not feel nervous', whereas an indirect suggestion is less authoritative and leaves an opportunity for interpretation. For example, 'When you are in front of the audience, you *might find* yourself feeling even more confident'. The preceding example follows the indirect method as both the specific time and level of self-confidence is left unspecified. It might be made even more indirect by saying, 'When you come to a decision to speak in public, you may find it appealing how your feelings have changed.' The choice of speaking in front of the audience, the exact time, and the likely responses to the whole process are framed, but imprecise language gives the client opportunity to fill in the finer details.

Let's use these examples in the same format in the last heading for the Meta Model.

Distortions

Presuppositions

Presupposition refers to an assumption whereby the truth is taken for granted. As we stated in the previous section, negation of an expression does not change its presuppositions. (You may want to skip this paragraph if you got it completely in the last section.) *I want to do it again* and *I don't want to do it again* both mean that the subject has done it already one or more times; *My school is good* and *my school is not good* both mean that the subject has a school to go to. In this respect, presupposition is distinguished from entailment and implication. For example, *the president was assassinated* entails that the president is dead, but if the expression is negated, the entailment is not necessarily true.

> Example: 'Don't even think about not learning in this class.' 'Some of you may learn quickly. Others will learn at their own pace, some of you may not learn as quickly' (all of the previous sentence implies learning, even though 'not' has been used ... it also provides for the listener to fill in the gaps about learning).

Have a go at drafting your own example:

Powerful language patterns

The Milton Model language patterns encourage the listener to move away from detail and content and move to higher levels of thinking and deeper states of mind. Some patterns are used to establish a relaxed state for thinking (or downtime or relaxation in the body). Other patterns are used to loosen the listener's model of the world from which they are expressing their current behaviours and to consider a more expansive interpretation of what is possible.

You will notice that many of these language patterns are identical to those of the Meta Model. The difference being that, for the Meta Model, the client is being vague and we ask specific questions to assist him in getting clarity on his issue/problem. For the Milton Model, we use some of the same language patterns, but this time we wish to be vague so that the client can easily go into trance and/or from the vague suggestions choose a suggested course of action that will address his own problem/issue.

Here are a few patterns that you can begin to learn if you so wish. It may be easier to take one or a few and learn/use them to begin with, before using the others.

Mind read

This is claiming to know another's thoughts or feelings without specifying how you came to that knowledge. You could use this in a class situation when you want to enter into discussion without disagreeing on something you actually don't agree on. For example, 'I know that you believe ...' or 'I know you're thinking ...', then just add whatever content is apparent. Once you have 'paced' their world, you can start to lead. (Pacing is a process where you stay at someone else's speed until you can lead on ... a bit like dancing with a new partner.)

The mind read means that you make a calculated guess about what they could possibly be thinking, without doubt and then report it. Generally, a speaker can make an educated guess about the listener's internal experience to build credibility and deepen rapport. Make sure the statement cannot be refuted, such as in the following:

'I know you are wondering how much you will learn from this class.'

Or (depending on the class), 'You may be wondering how long until the next break!'

'You may be curious about the teaching styles we will use this term.' (Whether they will know it or not, the listener has to go and 'try it on', therefore the deep mind will be considering teaching styles, learning, etc.)

We must be cautious to keep our references as general as possible. If specific details clash with the listener's thoughts, it will disrupt his or her attention.

Have a go at drafting your own example:

Lost performative

This is expressing value judgements without identifying the one doing the judging. 'Breathing is good', 'Learning is good', 'Exams are good'. None of these is intrinsically true, yet if you leave out who may have said them, they sound plausible. You could couple this with a mind read, 'well as you all know, knowing history is good for you'. Then you go on talking while their deep mind is listening intently. The beauty here is that 'as you all know' is not exactly true … but when delivered well, it seems plausible and that's the whole idea (politicians use this with great effect).

Have a go at drafting your own example:

Cause–effect

This implies one thing leads to or causes another: that there is a sequence of cause/effect and a flow in time. Included are phrases such as 'If ..., then ...; As you ..., then you ...; Because ..., then ...'.

'If you are listening intently, then you can learn many things.'

'The occasional sounds and noises from outside can make you want to concentrate more on what's inside here.' Here you have words like makes, causes, forces, because and requires.

A linkage works by connecting a statement that is pacing something that is already occurring with a statement that leads the listener to some other (usually internal) experience.

> Have a go at drafting your own example:

Complex equivalence

This is language that links two things together as one. It's like cause and effect but there are no steps here, simply *this means this*: 'Physical exercise is healthy', 'Food is fantastic', 'Being here means that you can learn easily'. Even if that is not 'true' for everyone, it cannot really upset anyone because it's such a positive and great invitation!

> Have a go at drafting your own example:

Presupposition

The linguistic equivalent of assumptions: 'will you be changing your mind when you sit here in the learning chair?' It is assumed the person will change their attitude. What you have skilfully done is presuppose learning and that there's a special chair for it. We know it's not 'true' yet the pupils can actually get realities like that and act upon them.

> Have a go at drafting your own example:

Universal quantifier

Universal generalizations without a referential index: everyone; no one; all; every – 'Everyone knows that listening means learning', 'All the other classes do this'.

Of course nobody can really say that 'everyone knows', or that 'all people' do something, but it's powerful when used correctly to give the impression of power in numbers.

> Have a go at drafting your own example:

Modal operator

Words that refer to possibility or necessity or that reflect internal states of intensity tied to our rules in life: 'You should care for others' or 'You must resolve this issue'. They can be used to direct the listener's experience in a certain direction: 'That you *can* learn so easily is a good metaphor for everyone', 'What we *should* do is share this learning strategy with everyone we know ... well we don't *have to*, but it *could* be a good thing!' As you can see, modal operators act as go-betweens and push and pull us in directions, depending on how they are used.

> Have a go at drafting your own example:

Nominalization

Words which are formed as nouns and which are shorthand for processes: 'People can come to new understandings'. Here 'understandings' is used as a noun and is shorthand to describe the ongoing experience of 'understanding' or 'making sense of something'.

If I were to say 'you know that you can feel *confident* about some *learnings* from last weekend ...', it is much easier for you to agree than if I were to say 'you know that you can feel confident about unspecified noun structures from last week ...'. *Learnings* is an example of a nominalization. To nominalize something means to make a noun out of something intangible (as in the last section on Meta Model), which doesn't exist in a concrete sense (in NLP, we say any noun that you can't put in a wheelbarrow is a nominalization). In this example, the process of learning something is turned into a noun, *learnings*.

Unspecified verb

Implies action without describing how the action has/will take place: 'He caused the problem', 'People can learn easily in this environment'. There are a few things in this last sentence that are not clear: Which people? How can they learn easily? What do they learn easily? When phrases like these are used, the listener is forced to use his or her imagination to fill in the who's and how's. Again, these types of phrases are useful for pacing and leading. If the speaker becomes too specific it could mismatch the listener and break rapport or minimize influence.

'So take a moment and enjoy remembering some of the things you learned and did at the last class.'

> Have a go at drafting your own example:

Tag question

A question added at the end of a statement/question, designed to soften resistance. It is used to ratify to the listener that he has or will actually manifest the action. It has the structure of a question and often the tonality of a statement: 'Your perception of learning this is changing, *isn't it?*' It almost goes back and qualifies the previous statement, while the listener was not expecting it ... therefore the tag imbeds the sentence.

> Have a go at drafting your own example:

Lack of Referential Index

An expression without specific reference to any portion of the speaker's/listener's experience: 'People can change'. There is obviously a lot of information deleted in this last phrase. When delivered with authority and rapport, it goes in nicely.

> Have a go at drafting your own example:

Comparative deletion (unspecified comparison)

A comparison is made without specific reference to what or to whom it is being compared: 'You will enjoy it more' or 'That one is better'. You have to be careful when using these as pupils are notoriously competitive, so when you use the words *better* or *more*, be prepared for battle. You can use it to create a team effect, though, by stating that your class is better.

Have a go at drafting your own example:

Pace current experience

Using sensory-grounded, behaviourally specific information to describe current experience: 'You are reading this article', 'You are sitting here, watching the slides …', '…and as you look at the slides, you could notice you are becoming curious about the meanings here'. You have just used pacing current experience with a suggestion for their minds. These include as, while, during and when.

Basically, anything they are doing, just mention it. What happens is their sub-dominant mind goes into a learning state because you are pacing their current experience. No one can deny they are actually doing that, so you get compliance!

Have a go at drafting your own example:

Double bind

Invites choice within a larger context of 'no choice': 'Do you want to begin now or in a few moments? or 'Are you going to be quieter before or after you sit down?' In teaching (or as parents) you have to love these double binds.

> Have a go at drafting your own example:

Embedded commands

This is a command that forms part of a larger sentence that is marked by using 'italics' or a subtle change in voice tonality or body language and is picked up by the reader's or listener's deep mind: 'I will not suggest to you that *learning is easy*' or 'Some people may have said it's not *easy*: well I'm not here to tell you this is *easy*, it's up to you to make up your own minds.' Notice that here, using 'not' will make no difference to hearing the *easy* part (see section on using 'not' effectively on page 131 of 'Setting goals for younger people', Chapter 6).

> Have a go at drafting your own example:

Conversational postulates

These are questions that operate at multiple levels. Although they require only a simple yes or no answer, they invite you to engage in an activity in some way. Often they contain an embedded command: 'Can you open the book at page 15?' or 'You might want to take out your notebooks for this one'. This simple language pattern displaces authority. Putting *'may want'* to, or *'you might'*, takes the challenge away from *'do this now!'*. Of course *'do this now!'* will work for some pupils.

Have a go at drafting your own example:

Extended quote

A rambling context for the delivery of information that may be in the format of a command.

> 'Many years ago, I remember meeting a wise old teacher who taught me many useful things. I cherished all of his advice. That was when I was younger, like you, yes I was younger you know. I loved the subject of … … and I remember that teacher saying to me one particular day *learning is all about listening*.'

When the mind has been preoccupied with a rambling story, you put in the part you want them to hear. *Remember the mind is always listening!*

Have a go at drafting your own example:

Selectional restriction violation

Attributing intelligence or animation to inanimate objects: 'Your chair can support you as you make these changes'; 'Your diary tells interesting tales'; 'The walls have ears'; 'The results tell us'; 'Your pen can know what to write before you even know it'. Of course walls don't really have ears, but when you say these types of phrases, the mind becomes interested in the ambiguity and therefore you can make them work to your advantage. Young minds are more flexible than older ones, generally, so you can apportion attributes to inanimate objects and make them do things for you!

> Have a go at drafting your own example:
>
>
>
>
>
>
>

Ambiguity: lack of specificity

(a) *Phonological:*

'your' and 'you're' – same sound, different meaning.

'here' and 'hear' – example: 'you are here, hearing different sounds in the classroom'; 'there was a bear, bearing down on me'.

(b) *Syntactic:* more than one possible meaning: 'they are teaching teachers' (so are they teachers that are teaching, or is someone teaching teachers?).

Or 'they are a class above' (so are they better than someone else, or are they literally in a class above?).

Or 'the pupils are getting smaller' (which pupils, eyes or in class?). Or 'they are visiting relatives'.

The syntax is uncertain within the context, i.e. adjectives, verbs or nouns?

(c) *Scope:*

'Speaking to you as a learner . . .' (who is the learner?).

'Or talking to you as a child. . .' (who is the child, them or you?). 'The old men and women . . .'

The context does not reveal the scope to which a verb or modifier applies.

(d) *Punctuation:* is unexpected and does not 'follow the rules', i.e. improper pauses, rambling sentences, incomplete sentences – all of which ultimately force the listener to 'mind read'.

"Hand me your watch how quickly you go into laughter." "notice that you're hand ... in hand with this class today ..."

> Have a go at drafting your own example:

Utilization

Takes advantage of everything in the listener's experience (both internal and external environments) to support the intention of the speaker. Pupil says: 'I don't understand.' Response: 'That's right ... you don't understand, yet, but now you've taken the time to ask me that question the information can easily fall comfortably into place.' Or perhaps while working with a class, one of your colleagues mistakenly opens a door. Instead of getting frustrated and annoyed with your colleague, you could say to your pupils, 'You may have heard a door opening and let this be an opportunity to invite new ideas and thoughts into your life.'

> Have a go at drafting your own example:

The Milton Model really is a very powerful tool.

Activity to try out

Take one pattern a day and use it in your class. See what effects it has when you use it with volition and notice what your intent was in using it and whether you achieved that or not.

Journal questions to consider

- What is the purpose of the Milton Model?
- When would you use this as opposed to the Meta Model?
- What is a dominant and deep mind and why is it useful to know this?

NLP in schools – language of persuasion

Now you have the basics in being able to traverse from the abstract to the very specific through language, we can get to grips with how to use your communication skills naturally in conversation.

One of the most powerful tools you have available to you is already at your finger tips – questions!

Questions

Questions allow your pupils to discover learnings for themselves and give their brains a chance to check all alcoves for associations. It's these association areas that, when developed, will lead to a person expanding their vocabulary in a given subject. Therefore, the better and more open ended your questions are, the more quality thinking time you're giving the pupils. Among new teachers, not leaving sufficient time after asking searching questions happens more frequently than is the case among established teachers (Rowe 1986).

Questions also allow you to control the classroom more powerfully. The pupils know that they are being given the floor. Even if they don't have the answers, they know they are being given the power to decide and contribute, and even win! So asking open-ended questions will give you time and space, and give them power. Not a bad trade off!

Common reasons teachers give for using questioning are, in order of perceived importance (Teaching and Learning Research Programme (TLRP)):

- encouraging thought and understanding of ideas
- checking understanding, knowledge and skills
- gaining attention to task, warming-up, moving towards a specific teaching point
- information, recall, review, revision, reinforcement.

In practice, though, we may find that our questions to pupils tend to be concerned with recalling facts:

Your evidence:
Gathering evidence about the way you interact with your pupils can help you to develop your pupils' thinking and understanding. One way you could do this would be to record a teaching session on audiotape. When you listen to the tape, you could record how often you ask questions designed to:

- recall factual information (e.g. 'Where is Ethiopia?')
- gain attention (e.g. 'Are you listening Wayne?')
- check understanding (e.g. 'Why do you think that?')
- encourage thought (e.g. 'What do you really think happened?').

What do you notice about the kind of questions you use with your pupils? What other kinds of questions can you dream up that can cause these good learning states to occur in the class? Think about a subject like Romeo and Juliet. What questions can you ask a class that gets them thinking? How about this for example:

'What is the relationship between Romeo and Juliet?' Some may say, 'friends', others may say 'lovers', and an abstract answer may be 'losers!'.

OK, so now you can open it up a bit:

'What's the purpose of this story, or what's the big picture here . . . what's going on?'

Which can lead you on to ask:

'Where in your life do you see the same thing happening that happened in the story?'

So, this was an example but perhaps you already use this approach and way of working a classroom . . . if so, well done!

Yet, perhaps you feel you aren't able to manage a room well. If this is the case, there may be reasons which may well be able to be resolved through your excellent speaking and listening.

1. *Insufficient rapport:* As dealt with in the chapter on rapport, you'll need to sort out the rapport leaders (the ring leaders) in the room and match and mirror (go into their world) and get respect. If this isn't possible the task will be harder, but still manageable.

2. *Not enough motivation to be learning the subject:* If this is the case, just add in *why* the subject will help them and how. How does this subject relate to their lives? If you don't know, spend a few minutes by yourself realizing how it does. If you can't come up with an answer or two, then you may have a reason why the class is not engaged ... and neither are you!

3. *Not engaging the class enough with questions:* Pupils are there to learn. They want to be engaged and also to know they exist! Asking questions enables them to realize they can get attention from applying thought to themselves and that's useful for you as well. Mercer and Littleton (2007) emphasize the importance of genuine dialogue to children's learning and development.

Try this:

You might like to see if you can increase the number of questions you ask that check your pupils' understanding and encourage them to think and reflect.

Would you find it helpful to work with a colleague to devise and practise asking such higher-order questions? Afterwards, you could record another of your lessons to see whether you used more higher-order questions with your pupils.

What about pupils asking questions?

When teachers are asked what strategies they use to teach reading comprehension, most say that the use of direct oral questioning is an important one. Classroom observation bears this out. Teachers more often use direct oral questioning to teach reading comprehension than any other strategy – perhaps as much as 70 per cent of the time, according to one study (TLRP).

Yet pupils rarely seem to ask questions and it is rare for teachers to explicitly suggest that pupils might find this helpful or to give them opportunities to practise asking questions for themselves. Few teachers (only 2 per cent in one study) mention supporting pupil's understanding by encouraging them to form their own questions.

You might like to explore patterns of asking questions within your own class-room, in order to see whether there is room for pupils to take a more active role in the activity.

You could record a lesson and then choose three five-minute periods (perhaps at the beginning, middle and end of the lesson) to find out more about who asks what in your classroom. Make a note of any questions asked during each period, as well as: who asked the question, and who answered. If pupils asked a question, was this related to the text? What was the purpose of each question?

A practise for you

Having sampled the questions used within a teaching session in your class, you could analyse the data in more detail. Can you see any patterns in who asks and who answers? Is there room for pupils to take a more active role in asking questions? Did any particular types of question seem to lead to deeper learning conversations?

You could discuss the findings you obtained from your pupils' current experiences with a colleague and work together to design or refine particularly effective questions that you might ask, or to plan how you could experiment with changing patterns of questioning in your class.

So what's in the future for you? What you'll begin to find is that with open-ended questions, coupled alongside your new skills to be able to use abstract language and specific language one-to-one and as a class, you will be in control of the space as never before.

So, in how many ways can you begin to imagine what teaching can be like now, just as a possibility?

An advanced use of languaging and questioning for pupils with learning and behavioural difficulties

When working with young people who have learning or behavioural difficulties and whilst trying to attend to the special needs of every young person, we sometimes need to delve far deeper into specific issues. The skills discussed in this book so far are all useful in a general sense in the classroom as well as in an individual sense with young people; however, sometimes we find ourselves having to work more individually. Below is a format for doing this with the top end of Key Stage 2, Key Stage 3 and 4. These are quite advanced ways of using language, so if you are not there yet, continue with using what you have learned and perhaps come back to these at a later time.

While asking these questions use all the rapport skills and calibration discussed previously in the book and watch out for unconscious signals telling you when the young person is congruent with what they are saying or not.

You may know the young person very well already, in which case you have a good start point, but you may feel you need to know the young person even better. Most people like to talk about things they enjoy doing, so perhaps you can introduce a topic you know they are interested in and get them talking about it. I have found that when working with particularly difficult and unforthcoming young people, using a simple pack of cards for a game of snap or rummy, to divert attention from the conversation, can provide opportunity for discussion to begin. You may even learn a few tricks from the kids – I have! Cards are good because they can be in your pocket at any time, ready for use. During seven years in advisory work I have never had a child say no to a game of cards, and certainly some of the best conversations came over a game.

So now you have the scene. You are in a quiet place having a game of cards, looking like you aren't doing any work, when in fact you are doing some very important work. For the first two or three games, you talk around the young person's interests, whatever they may be. You talk about the things they are good at – by this time you may have been able to dispense with the cards and you may even be able to make a note of the things that they are good at in some way, either in a notebook, or better still, on a mind-map so that they can see what you are writing, or even better, they draw it out themselves. You bring the subject round to the things they do that are a problem to them, the behaviours or learning strategies that cause difficulty. You then pose questions, such as the following, to tease out how they know they have a problem:

When do you do it? When don't you do it?
Where do you do it? Where don't you do it?
How do you do it? How don't you do it?
What do you do? What don't you do?

If this problem disappeared for ever right now, how would you know it has gone?
What would you see, hear, feel, smell?

So, for example, if during the course of your conversation you came up with the problem 'walking out of the classroom and out of school', you might continue with a conversation something like this:

'When do you do it?' *'When I want to.'*
'Okay, so when do you want to do it, specifically? Is it all lessons . . . or just some?' *'No, not all, just some.'*
'Which?' *'One's with Mrs Jones.'*
'Okay, so when don't you do it?' *'In the other lessons.'*
'What, none others?' *'Well, I do it in some others as well, Mrs Hall and Mr Goode, I can't stand him.'*
'Okay, so you do it in Mrs Jones's, Mrs Hall's and Mr Goode's lessons but not in all others?' *'Yeah.'*
'Do you have all your lessons with these teachers in the same rooms?' *'Yes.'* (negates *where* questions)
'Can I ask you again . . . how do you do "room leaving"?' *'What do you mean?'*
'Well, how exactly do you do it, show me, tell me?' *'I just get up and walk out.'*
'You just get up at any time?' *'No, its usually when I've been in there a bit and I get bored and just think, oh sod it, I'm not staying here and I just get up and go out, or sometimes I might have got told off about something, that's all the time really.'*
'How don't you do "room leaving"?' *'What do you mean?'*

'Well, if you don't leave the room, what does it look like, what would I see?' *'I'd just be sitting there.'*

'When you are sitting there, what do you do?' *'I sit and get on with my work.'*

'What don't you do?' *'Mess about, shout out, walk about the room, that kind of thing.'*

'If this problem disappeared right now for good, how would you know it had gone?' *'I suppose I'd sit in my seat, do my work, get on without talking and shouting out, be able to do my work, get on well at school.'*

At this point you could go on, but in reality you will probably find that both of you are getting quite exhausted, so it may be that you need to carry on at another time. You may find that the young person simply highlighting for themselves how things would be if the problem disappeared may enable their deep mind to start working on the issue. The language you have been using has been subtly suggesting that the behaviour can go away and the mind has envisioned a different way of being.

In a follow up session, after reminding the young person of the previous discussions if you felt it was necessary, you could proceed with the following questions:

If the (leaving the room) problem did go away overnight, what wouldn't you have that you do have now?

What is leaving the room stopping you from doing that if it went away you would have to do?

What else are you not doing because you leave the room?

What are you doing that you enjoy because of leaving the room that you would have to stop doing when you had stopped leaving the room?

It may be that at this point a totally new issue comes up, which in fact is driving the obvious problem behaviour or ineffective learning strategy. You can then look at this in a couple of ways: either it has exposed a need that is not being met and needs to be met in an alternative way, in which case you and the young person can work out a way together to do that; or it has exposed an issue that the young person would like to do something about and to change themselves – maybe they have a limiting belief that they would like to get rid of. If this is the case, you can work together to set goals as described in Chapter 6.

Now you try!

> You pose the following questions to tease out how they know they have a problem
>
>
> When do you do it?

Okay, so when do you want to do it, specifically? Is it all lessons ... or just some?

Which?

Okay, so when don't you do it?

Any other time?

Okay, so you ... (rephrase to show you have been listening and understanding)

Where do you do it?

Anywhere else?

So you ... (reiterate where behaviour occurs)

Where don't you do it?

Anywhere else?

So you don't ... (reiterate where behaviour occurs)

How do you do '(the problem)'?

Well, how exactly do you do it, show me, tell me?

You just do this any time?

How don't you do '(the problem)?

What would I see?

What don't you do when you aren't doing it?

If this problem disappeared right now for good, how would you know it had gone?

In a follow-up session, after reminding the young person of the previous discussions if you felt it was necessary, you could proceed with the following questions:

If the problem did go away overnight, what wouldn't you have that you do have now?

What is (the problem) stopping you from doing, that if it went away you would have to do?

What else are you not doing because you (do the problem)?

What are you doing that you enjoy because of (the problem) that you will have to stop doing when you have stopped (the problem)?

Then, if the pupil has 'turned the corner' you could go on to goal setting (see Chapter 6).

Journal reflections

What is your gut reaction to the Meta and Milton models?

Chapter 5 quiz

	True	False	Maybe
1. Our language is distorted, deleted and generalized by our deep mind			
2. The Meta Model is a collection of vague statements			
3. Effective challenging of a person's limiting language needs to be done patiently			
4. The Meta Model enables you to identify when a person is using sloppy thinking			
5. Awareness of sloppy thinking enables you to reduce misunderstandings and make communication clearer			
6. Distortion is the key to creativity			
7. A lost performative recovers the choice			
8. Complex equivalence means two experiences are interpreted as being synonymous			
9. The question 'how specifically?' is great for clarifying sloppy thinking			
10. The Milton Model uses vague language to your advantage			
11. The Milton Model patterns should be used to confuse everyone			
12. Embedded commands can be used to place important points in the class			
13. The Milton Model and Meta Model are two distinct and exclusive systems			

Answers and discussion can be found on page 144.

6   Setting goals

This last chapter is about thinking about the future, so we are looking at goal setting.

For me, gone are the days when setting goals was a dry and arduous task. These days I do not plant seeds unless I know the ground is fertile and I get the feeling of fun and expectancy beforehand!

I don't know how many seminars and courses I have been on where goal setting was presented as a fragmented and an unintergrated process, seemingly to please the person running the training. Put it like this (and this may be a relief to some of you), if the visions do not have a huge degree of synchronicity to a person's life and aspirations, the goals do not work! So, as you read through this chapter, bear it in mind. If you are the person who is responsible for fulfilling the demands, you'd better want to be toiling the soil or those seeds won't grow.

Further to the analogy of gardening, if you think of yourself as a gardener, a landscape gardener, and you're looking out onto a fairly empty piece of land, this will be akin to the process of looking into the future and beginning to design something from nothing. The way you toil the soil will be the way you think about things. Your ability to plan and direct focus, focusing your attention on what you really want, will be the key to being able to hold and maintain a positive, lasting focal point. Your knowing what and when to take out of the land what's not needed will be your way of making space for the seeds which are your thoughts and ideas, which will bear fruit in the future.

Over many years of dedicated goal setting and struggling to make those goals, I have come to the conclusion that this area is one of the most underrated, yet powerful, if dealt with responsibly and with passion. It would make more difference than almost any other area that you choose to work on.

Most people have goals as something they *have to* attain, and use words like *should, must, have to, it's right*, or *got to have it* in their vocabulary. This is a self-defeating target in itself. Our body and our mind are not slaves, and yet we try to force them to achieve things that aren't wholesome and passionate, and then the body and the mind rejects them somehow or other, either through some drama or another, getting ill, accidents, or any other way that the body and mind can trip one up. If you try and force yourself with no self-motivation behind the goals, it's just the same as trying to make a full tide an ebb tide ... pretty useless!

Don't get me wrong here! If you know that running a marathon would be good for you, yet you know it's going to be a huge pull on your resources and ever so tough, it can still be good for self-motivation and is most probably a worthwhile proposition.

Finding the right goals for you

So how do you find the right goals for you that come from natural motivation?

As a teacher, you already will have some parameters which you work from or to. These are sometimes set by other people, just by default. You are already under the persuasion of somebody else's ideas and influences but, of course, as a teacher you've already bought into the idea of education and belonging to a large group, so you consider yourself in a team and working with the team. In these circumstances, you can look at the goals that you already have in terms of the class and then look for some other goals that would give you tremendous satisfaction as a teacher, both for yourself and for your pupils. There are more ambiguous goals and more abstract goals that you can look at as opposed to just getting the results that you want your pupils to get.

One thing to bear in mind is that your pupils are mostly responsible for getting their own results, and you're merely assisting them. So you cannot be completely responsible for everything that they are getting. Yet, you can have some degree of control over the feel of the class and passion of a class, setting this as one of your own performance goals, along with goals relating to your pupils' levels of achievement

The power of your focus is not quantifiable. From my experience, you are infinitely powerful. You have more dynamic power within you than you can possibly imagine.

I was once working in the business sector with a man who was a sports journalist and also a trader on the stock market. After some really good productive work we did on visioning his business world, he came to me with regard to his relationships, about the ideal relationship that he wanted. I did a bit of basic NLP goal setting with him, which I will show you in a moment, and then asked him when and where he wanted this relationship to occur. He told me he wanted it to be happening right now! Well, he looked across at me, so I ducked as I was the only other person in the room at the time. I said, 'Now!' We both laughed.

I was later to realize the bigger joke, that really was about to happen. We set a more reasonable time of two weeks for him to meet a particular person. About a month later, he called very excitedly. I asked them how it was going. He said he had already found the person that we put into his goals and he was living in a house that he had visioned in our session a few weeks earlier.

I asked him when this has happened. I almost fell off my chair when he told me. He said, when he got home, the very same day that we had been doing the exercise, there was a message for him, an email from a woman, whom he subsequently met. It turned out to be exactly the partner that we had been talking about (creating) in our session! They ended up living together in a very short space of time. So when he was sitting in my front room, and he said the word *now*, literally it was already happening!

This worked just as powerfully for myself when I was training in Sweden. After finishing an NLP training course, I sat with my Swedish friend Susanne in a cafe. We had a quiet chat about the future. Of course we were both in a very powerful state. Not a problem or care in the world and very full of positive energy. Talking with Susanne, I told her that the next thing I wanted in life was to be working with very influential people, people who make decisions about how the country is run or how the world is run in some way, but I then thought little more about it. Within three days I had a call from the Cabinet Office in Whitehall, asking me to tender for training the staff at the Cabinet Office. I won that tender, and we delivered training to the Cabinet office staff and subsequently I began coaching one-to-one for a period of time! How's that for a quick turnaround of goals?

From what we know about goals, visualizing them and experiencing them before they actually happen gives your mind and your body a fantastic opportunity to check on all the aspects and the motivation that sits behind them.

In the book, *The Holographic Universe* (Talbot 1996), it is shown how experiments undertaken with visualizations and role-playing before a specific goal is attained is more effective than the physical training itself. In an experiment conducted with basketball teams, the teams that spent the most time visualizing the goals were the most effective and won more games than the other teams (of the same quality), that went out and physically practised as much as possible without as much visualization.

Even though this is a proven fact, it's not just about the visualization. The questions that follow will give you the chance to filter out unwanted parts of a particular goal, which is the first stage to any successful visioning. Even though the filtering questions are just words on a page, the questions have been specifically chosen and phrased in a way that gets the whole of your nervous system to jump to attention. They are contrast frames, tests, and checks, internally to externally, to align them from your inner world to your outer world.

Whenever I'm working with pupils, the very first thing that I'm interested in and curious about is what they think they want to achieve. It's a very special time, when a learner is giving you their map of the world and their reality. It's a time when, as the teacher, or the learning provider, you have the chance to contribute to their world in a way that takes a goal that may not be realistic and makes it realistic. To take a goal that may not be achievable and make it achievable. Or take a goal that was not really their goal in the first place and make it really theirs, something that they can be passionate about, and *own*.

Now, even though some people may be successful in their own right, at this point I want to emphasize that they are inherently no different from anybody else on the planet. They have no special abilities above and beyond anybody else; yet what happens with successful people is that they follow the *laws of attraction* and use the process of goal setting with this is mind.

Before we get into the filter questions, let's briefly talk about natural passion. The passion that sits behind the goal – that feeling of motivation – is much more important than the goal itself. The goal is actually driven by the feeling by motivation. If that isn't there, it would like be trying to push a car up a hill. Goals are not slaves to be whipped and held to be wrong if they don't work. They are simply vehicles which wait for the right person, with the right motivation, to assist them in going forward.

Firstly, we need to filter out anything about the goals which are not congruent or aligned to the person. That's very important! If we defer to the gardening analogy, this is the process of removing the unwanted weeds, rocks, and the like. That's where we can reconnect to our passion again if it was missing.

The series of questions that follows enables one to filter out anything which is not completely true about the goal, or set of goals, in your life. I underline that, what is even more important than using these questions, is getting in touch with what you really want, which will leave you with what you are passionate about in life, about being a teacher, and about what you want to achieve while being at the school and being in the classroom.

When you're working with pupils, you may have to edit this filter system, taking into consideration the age of the pupil and what you know of their goals already.

Okay, I think it's time for you to go ahead and experience this. Perhaps you can use this set of questions to filter out what you consider to be important to you as you go through your career and your lessons or classes. You can use it for any goal at any time, so go ahead and pick a goal that you are really passionate or think you're passionate about achieving and use these questions to filter that goal into something that you will be willing to commit to within a particular time frame.

Begin by asking yourself: 'How is it possible that I (they) don't have it now?'

1. **Stated in the positive**

What specifically do you want?

2. **Specify present situation**

Where are you now? (Talk about this in the first person as if it's happening now.)

3. **Specify outcome**

What will you see, hear, feel, etc., when you have it?

4. **Specify evidence procedure**

How will you know when you have it?

5. **Is it congruently desirable?**

> What will this outcome get for you or allow you to do?

6. **Is it self-initiated and/or self-maintained?**

> Can you be responsible for the outcome, or is it someone else? (If the answer is no, it's not your goal at all.)

7. **Is it appropriately contextualized?**

> Where, when, how, and with who do you want it?

8. **What resources are needed?**

> What do you have now, and what do you need to get your outcome?

Have you ever had or done this before? (Ask this to give some reality.)

Do you know anyone who has?

Can you act as if you have it? (If they really can't get into the state.)

9. **Is it ecological?**

For what purpose do you want this?

What will you gain or lose if you have it?

The four questions on page 130, are really mind-twisters – it's not important that you know everything about these questions, albeit their origin is Rene Descartes, who used questions very similar to these to filter out mathematical equations and to prove theorems. Of course he was a fantastic philosopher as well, and groups of people used to use these questions to improve their thinking capacity and to improve their standards of learning as early as in the fifteenth century. When you're using these four questions it's not important that you get completely accurate answers, but it is important that you fully consider the question when you're looking at your goal or considering your goal.

(A) What *will* happen if you get it?

(B) What *won't* happen if you get it?

(C) What *will* happen if you *don't* get it?

(D) What *won't* happen if you *don't* get it?

Setting goals with younger people

Using the previous model may be too complex (or not necessary) for some ages of pupils. With regard to this, an alternative, simpler method is the process below, called **SMART** goals.

Specific Simple

Measurable Meaningful to you

As if now/Achievable

Realistic Responsible/Ecological

Timed/Towards What You Want

Let's just run through this model. **S** is for simple and specific, simply meaning that the goal is very easy for anyone to understand. It is so easy, you could fit one goal into one picture or perhaps even one sentence. The simpler the goal is in explanation, the more powerfully your whole system can focus on it.

M is for *meaningful* to you. Meaningful, as we have stated earlier, is one of the most important factors in setting a goal. The book *Think and Grow Rich* by Napoleon Hill, was written in the 1930s, and commissioned by Dale Carnegie to find out what makes rich and famous people tick. Napoleon Hill discovered that there are a finite number of predictable elements that make goals and success happen. He interviewed rich and famous people over a period of 25 years, and came out with a recipe for anyone to use. One of those predictable elements was passion!

M also stands for measurable. If I were going to France, I'd need a map and a way of measuring distance, so I could keep on track all the way.

A stands for achievable, which means that the person realizes that they really can do a particular thing and that it's not just a pipe dream.

A is also for *as if now*. This means that when you're constructing a goal do use language in the present tense. For instance, 'I am now looking at the results of my exams. I am seeing I have got the grade XYZ that I wanted.' This gives the mind a real sign that this is happening and it isn't past or future tense. It really is happening now!

R is for realistic and responsible. Both of these words mean that the goal has to affect a wider audience than just the person themselves. In this way, the goal has far more power and is much more far-reaching.

T is for *timed* and you will, of course, be used to having a set time and time limits for projects and subjects and a set curriculum! Yet if you're setting goals for yourself or with others and there's a time limit placed on it, it indicates the urgency of the goal to the whole of your system. If you think of the whole of your system as a community in itself, you're really telling the community when things need to be done by. So the whole system can work as a whole to gain you what you want in the least amount of time possible.

T is also for *towards*. This piece in goal setting is commonly the bit most people miss out completely when verbalizing an action or goal. Think of it this way: your deeper mind (or unconscious mind), cannot process negatives very easily; so, in other words, if you're telling somebody not to do something, what do you think they're then going to focus on? Let me show the above in the form of an experiment. In one moment, I'm going to ask you ***not*** to think about something. Now, I have already let you know that I'm going to do this with you, so you're completely and utterly prepared to ***not*** to think about something when I give you the suggestion. So here we go, right now, ***don't*** think of a banana with melted chocolate over the top of it. So, what happened? Well, of course, you probably had to go inside and think about that very thing, or have a picture of or even a feeling of the banana with melted chocolate (perhaps you're hungry right now!).

Research into how the mind works proves that you have to consider something even if ***not*** is said before it. This is as crucial as is a parent, teacher or a trainer when it comes to giving instructions to pupils. If you keep telling them *not* to do something, then where do you think the focus will be? Perhaps that's why we've got so many naughty kids! Whether we are teachers or trainers, we need to keep our language focused on the outcome, not the problem, and on what we *do* want them to do. So, keep the focus as clearly as possible on what you want the person to do regarding any pictures, sounds, feelings and outlines.

Of course, sometimes it is necessary to say don't do something, but then just do it with the correct percentage for instance, if you don't want them to do something tell them what you don't want them to do, but emphasize that on a 3-1 ratio, what you do want them to do. That way, they have a clear crystal focus about what they do want. For instance, if a pupil is worried about their exams, what do you think they're focusing on? Well, some people are motivated by the stick, so they are thinking, '*I don't want to fail*', and that may give them some purchase on motivating themselves and doing more work, except that creates quite a stressful environment internally.

If they are using the language pattern *I don't want to fail*, what do you think they're focusing on? Well, of course, the focus is completely on failing! Sometimes the prospect of failure may wake up pupils to the motivation that's behind it, and it's always the motivation behind it that you want to find. And if you do have to use negative language, then use it consciously to get pupils motivated. Then, when you have inspired the pupil to be motivated, then you can start to look at where they *do* want to go with you and what they really do want.

It's so common in our culture to think of what we don't want that it's almost second nature. From now on, keeping in mind how to positively set goals will make the outcomes so much easier for you and your pupils!

When using either of the above processes, the last advanced piece is how to set a goal in stone. What you'll need to do is make a picture or a representation of the final outcome of what they want to achieve. The final outcome may be the grade that they're looking for or the result they want from a particular exam, or what they want from their class work during the period.

When they have used any of the above processes, they should have a very clear representation of exactly what they do want. The next thing is to get them to project forward and decide the time when they want to achieve it. And if they've got a mental diary in their mind, or a mental calendar, get them to places in that internal representation or picture (bear in mind some people do not make pictures as well as others, so let them know they can do this by feelings or sounds as well) with all the feelings pictures, sounds, colours and words that go with it.

If appropriate, get them to close their eyes, go inside, and then visualize this happening, and then turn the colour and brightness up, turn the feelings and sounds up and make the picture as attractive as possible, while they put it into the internal diary or calendar at the exact time they want this to happen.

This acts as an incredibly powerful anchor and will allow their learning to be like an escalator or a fast track to aid them to exactly where they're going. You will find that this way of setting goals is more powerful than you can possibly imagine. I use it time after time with pupils, in the training room and on myself!

This is the new way I now use to set goals. It's much more natural and avoids those aggressive or pushy words. You can force agendas and the goal may be achieved, but if this does happen it will have been very stressful. It's much better to have fewer goals with more passion, or even one goal with a lot of passion, because there will be more learning and more understanding, more of yourself there.

Questions for your journal

- What have you just learned about setting goals?
- How will you put this into your schedule for yourself and your pupils?
- What is the first smallest step you can make today to implement this way at looking at success?
- What are your own goals for the future?

- What do you have to complete in your daily life so that you can start to experience your future looking good?

List out everything in your life that needs tidying up; this might include bills that have to be paid, cleaning, friends who you haven't called, projects you haven't finished, dreams that you haven't given up on but haven't done anything about, if fact anything that isn't yet complete and is hanging around. List out all of these incompletions and set about completing them (yes I know it may take a while)!

Conclusion

Now you have completed your workbook and you have a basic knowledge of NLP. You are likely to feel you have only seen or felt the tip of the iceberg and that is true. NLP is a vast array of practical skills, and to learn these properly you need to be with others who are learning and practising too, but your deep mind has started the process. Now you can go on and complete some practical training to become an excellent practitioner – after all, being an excellent practitioner is what we all want to be, isn't it?

Chapter 6 quiz

	True	False	Maybe
1. Goal setting is as much about what you decide not to do as what you decide to do			
2. Goals are most attainable when they come from natural motivation			
3. Visualizing your goal enables you to check if you are congruent with the goal			
4. The first question to ask when goal setting is 'how is it possible I don't have what I want already?'			
5. It is OK to set targets for children in school stating behaviours we don't want them to do			

Answers and discussion can be found on page 145.

Neuro-Linguistic Programming glossary

This glossary is by no means exhaustive, but it does give a few short definitions of some NLP terms and should make the language of NLP a little easier to internalize. For a much more comprehensive glossary look at www.nlpworld.co.uk.

Accessing cues   Slight changes in breathing, posture, gestures and eye movements that show internal mental processing such as visualization, auditory and kinaesthetic activity. Watching out for these helps the observer assess the congruence of the actor with ideas presented to him.

Anchoring   The process of associating an internal response with an external trigger so that by applying a gesture, touch, sound or smell just before a state peaks, either in oneself or someone else, the anchored state can be reactivated by reapplying that gesture, touch, sound or smell.

Associated   Looking through your own eyes, hearing what you heard, feeling what you felt, smelling what you smelled as intensely as if you were actually there is associating.

Away from One of the filters which describe how we make choices about situations. Some people are very 'away from' in that they like to move away from a situation rather than moving towards a more positive one. Knowing how children react in this way makes constructing behaviour programmes more effective because you can use carrots and sticks according to whether they respond to towards stimuli or away from.

Calibration   The skill of recognizing visible, auditory and kinaesthetic 'facts' from a person, rather than mind-reading their body language.

Congruence   When all of a person's internal beliefs, strategies, and behaviours are fully in agreement with their verbal output while communicating. Convincing people will appear normal and natural when their body language sits comfortably with what they are saying.

Content reframing   Changing your response to an experience by changing the meaning you give to it.

Context reframing   Taking an event to another place so that the meaning changes by that movement.

Deletion   A way of coping with the mass of information the brain is presented with every second. For instance, we all have deleted the mass of pixels that are all around us, all the time. The small stain on the desk is not noticed in the chaos of the class (if you are noticing it, then you are probably too relaxed)!

Deep Mind   *See* unconscious mind

Dissociation   Looking at your body from an outside position and experiencing the world from outside your own physical position so that you do not have the feelings you would have if you were actually there. Being able to be dispassionate about an emotional situation.

Distortion   A way the human brain copes with large amounts of information constantly bombarding it. Events are represented differently from the real world, making them fit in more easily with existing patterns. Teachers are experts at being able to distort the briefs given to them (which are sometimes impossible), to be able to make the results really happen!

Ecology   Ecology is the consideration of effects of changes that could happen if a goal is achieved. The ecology of a goal for instance would include family, partners, colleagues, as well as possible effects on the physical environment.

Embedded commands   Instructions that are subtly included in speech, but marked out by changing the voice tone (deeper and louder).

Future pace   The process of mentally rehearsing a situation to ensure a positive outcome.

Generalization   A way the brain copes with the mass of information it is presented with by taking a specific incident or behaviour and generalizing it across contexts.

Incongruence   A divided response indicating reservation and a not total commitment to an outcome. The words do not match the actions. The body does not reflect the speaking.

Intention   The purpose or outcome of any behaviour.

Internal representation   The pictures, sounds and feelings that we make on the inside; our thoughts. The way we store and sort our memories in a kind of mental map.

Lead system   The preferred representational system – visual, auditory, kinaesthetic – that takes information from the exterior. Usually outside conscious awareness. Can detect via someone's eye patterns.

Leading   The process of gaining sufficient rapport with another to lead their behaviour using both verbal and non-verbal communication to elicit a desired response from another person.

Matching   Adopting parts of another person's behaviour and language preferences to enhance rapport.

Meta Model   The Meta Model provides questions to elicit lost information which previously was distorted, generalized and deleted.

Metaphor   Stories, parables, analogies, allegories that enable the deep mind to understand new things. These methods tap directly into the deep mind, enabling learning through the deep mind.

Milton Model   The 'artfully vague' language used to induce confusion or uncertainty in another's listening. Used to bypass the conscious guards of disbelief. Based on the language used by hypnotherapist Milton H. Erickson M.D. It is the complement to the precise Meta Model, deliberately generalizing, distorting and deleting content.

Modelling   The process of observing, replicating and mapping the successful behaviours of other people.

Nominalization   A verb which has been turned into an abstract noun, e.g. 'learnings' is a nomilization because we have not defined the word before using it.

Outcomes   Goals or desired states that a person or organization aspires to achieve, framed in positive terms and within the individuals ambit.

Pacing   A method used by excellent communicators to quickly establish rapport by matching certain aspects of their behaviour to those of the person with whom they are communicating – a matching or mirroring of behaviour.

Perceptions   The half full/half empty glass. We can interpret this as: if you want more, it is half empty; if you have had enough, it is half full. We cannot change how much is in the glass, only the way we think about it.

Preferred/Primary Representation System   The representational system that an individual uses to express their internal world.

Presupposition A basic underlying assumption that is necessary for an internal representation to make sense, e.g. 'well you have done this before so you can easily do it again' presupposes you can. 'If you sit in this learning chair, learning becomes twice as fast.' As long as there is enough rapport for someone to consider a truth in what you are saying, then the presuppositions will work! Often a presupposition is outside a person's conscious awareness.

Rapport The establishment of trust, harmony, and cooperation in a relationship. Groups can be in rapport and show this by synchronized behaviour. Rapport can be gained by matching body language and behaviour.

Reframing (see also content reframing and context reframing) Changing the meaning of a situation by putting a different frame or perspective on one's thoughts about it, e.g. 'I have no money'. Challenge, 'compared to whom, the guy in the shop doorway?'

Resource Anything that adds to the achievement of an outcome, so it could be a belief, understanding, piece of knowledge. Any internal or external assistance. In NLP we tend to guide others to knowing they have access to all resources.

Sensory acuity The process of learning to make finer and more useful distinctions about the information we get from the world by attending to fine changes in physiology of another. Information that can be used to calibrate (make factual observations) on another.

Unconscious or deep mind (sub-dominant or 'not' the conscious mind) Mental processes outside conscious awareness. The majority of one's learning takes place in the deep mind, so, as teachers, it's a good idea to see how well you are relating to this area in your teaching skills. Also the conscious mind can only handle very small amounts of information, so you'll need to provide small packages to allow learning to occur. Either that, or learn how to use NLP more proficiently to access deeper areas of learning; more colourful, more sensory based, to appeal to the deep mind. For example, you can put across untold amounts of information in a metaphor as opposed to about five key points in plain, logical fact.

Chapter quiz answer sheets

Chapter 1 quiz

	True	False	Maybe
1. If you can control your mind, you can have the greatest influence over your own behaviour	x		
2. NLP is a theory-based discipline		x	
3. Modelling the way excellent communicators work can improve your communication skills	x		
4. Noticing a person's preferred communication style (Visual, Tactile, Auditory, Self talk) can assist you in gaining rapport *Always try to tune in to a person's preferred communication style and gain better rapport by using it, then you can start to take them with you into learning they could have been resistant to before*		x	
5. A good relationship in the classroom has no effect on learning *A good relationship is possibly THE MOST important thing you need in the classroom*		x	
6. NLP can help people overcome fears, anxieties and limitations *Many NLP techniques have been used to help people overcome problems*	x		
7. NLP has no place in the classroom, just in a theory class *NLP has EVERY place in the classroom, and even if you think you aren't using NLP you will be, but you could be using it even better if you read this book and go on suitable training*		x	
8. Rapport is the keystone of NLP	x		
9. Our reality is what we perceive it to be through our senses	x		
10. Presuppositions are simply convenient beliefs which are designed to see life through different glasses	x		

11. There is no link between the mind and your well being *There is more and more writing about the links between mind and body wellness that it is becoming something that cannot be ignored*		x	
12. There is no such thing as feedback only failure *In NLP we say 'There is no such thing as failure only feedback' meaning we can learn from every situation and experience*		x	
13. There are no resistant pupils, only inflexible teachers	x		
14. Flexibility achieves control *If you look at great entrepreneurs, they have been people who are able to adapt to situations and turn a disadvantage into an advantage*	x		
15. The meaning of your communication is the response that you get from others *Remember this is the feedback – if the feedback isn't what you want, change the way you deliver the message*	x		
16. In NLP we believe that people don't have enough resources to succeed so we need to supply them for others *In NLP we believe we have ALL of the resources we need within us and that human beings have incredible potential*		x	
17. No behaviour is wrong in itself, but it is not always the most appropriate behaviour for the context *This is a hard one to agree with sometimes, but if you think about behaviour abstractly you can argue that all behaviour has a positive intent, however it is the context which is wrong and that is often what we need to work on in school*	x		
18. NLP requires you to change your own behaviour before you can expect a change from anyone else *There is another saying 'if you always do what you've always done you'll always get what you've always got'. How true!*	x		

Chapter 2 quiz

	True	False	Maybe
1. Matching and mirroring is simply copying another person's traits, like a monkey		x	
2. Body language is more truthful than words when it comes to communication *We might think we know what people mean by their mannerisms, but the only reliable way to tell is to watch and calibrate because we are not all the same*		x	
3. Skin tone, head position, lip size, breathing rate are all conscious communication signals *They are UNCONSCIOUS signals and for this reason they are particularly useful in helping to read what a person is meaning because they are more truthful than what we say*		x	
4. You can use changes in voice tone to tell consistently if a person is happy or not. *The voice is very telling and if you calibrate on it without being confused by the other senses you can become very good at telling a person's mood from the voice alone*	x		
5. People will know immediately if you are matching or mirroring them *When you match and mirror with a little skill they should soon feel a sense of rapport developing without really being aware why*		x	
6. We delete pieces of information unconsciously to avoid over stimulation	x		
7. Eye patterns can tell you where a person has gone to sort information	x		
8. Knowing how a child's direction filter operates can help in planning behaviour programmes and using rewards or sanctions to motivate behaviour *This is a definite plus when planning behaviour programmes as it helps you to work out which direction a person is motivated in*	x		
9. Some pupils look for similarities and the familiar whilst others look for differences	x		

10. You can calibrate on what a person likes/dislikes and apply this to any other situation with this person	x		
11. The size of the chunks that you deliver information in the classroom are not important *Chunk size might not seem important but in fact getting it right can make a big difference to how people respond to information*		x	
12. The NLP three R's are Rapport Reduces Resistance *I like this reframe, don't you?*	x		

Chapter 3 quiz

	True	False	Maybe
1. Students learn more when instructed in styles different from their own representational style *Matching a person's representational style will enable you to gain rapport more quickly and to introduce learning more effectively*		x	
2. Knowing your own representational style (VAKOG) will help you modify your communication to match your pupils *You always need to know yourself to be able to communicate well with others. If you don't know what style you use, how can you amend it to match someone else's?*	x		
3. You can 'translate' from your language to that of another person by emulating their representational style *In its simplest form using phrases like 'I can see that you would prefer to do this another way' for a person who likes visual writing, or 'I hear what you are saying about this and maybe we could sound out another way to do it?' for an auditory person will tune in to them more effectively than using unpreferred styles*	x		

Statement			
4. If you are working with a child who is highly visual, slow down and modulate your voice more and really listen well *People who are visual often stand or sit with their heads and/or bodies erect, with their eyes up. They will be breathing from the top of their lungs. They often sit forward in their chair and tend to be organized, neat, well-groomed and orderly. They memorize by seeing pictures, and are less distracted by noise. They often have trouble remembering verbal instructions because their minds tend to wander. A visual person will be interested in how your programme **LOOKS**. Appearances are important to them. They are often thin and wiry.*		x	
5. When working with someone who is kinaesthetic, sit up high in your chair and breathe from the top of your lungs *People who are kinaesthetic will typically be breathing from the bottom of their lungs, so you'll see their stomach go in and out when they breathe. They often move and talk verrry slooowly. They respond to physical rewards, and touching. They also stand closer to people than a visual person. They memorize by doing or walking through something. They will be interested in your programme if it **FEELS RIGHT**.*		x	
6. When you gain rapport you experience a sense of knowing the other person *You will instinctively know when you are in rapport*	x		
7. To practise rapport skills choose a child in your class you get on really well with and match and mirror their mannerisms with respect *It's probably better to choose one you don't get on well with because the results will be more astonishing*			x
8. Simply changing the timbre of your voice can be enough to establish good rapport *It's good to try more than this, but if you are on the phone you really only have chunk size, subject matter and timbre*	x		
9. You cannot build rapport with a whole class *Group rapport can easily be gained by mirroring the feelings of the group*		x	
10. It is impossible to tell from a person's eye movements what they are thinking		x	
11. EMDR is a technique used to link different areas of the brain	x		

Chapter 4 quiz

	True	False	Maybe
1. Anchors should only be used on others in the classroom *Anchoring is an extremely useful method of putting people into the 'learning state', but you can also use them on yourself*		x	
2. Anchoring happens when a state is so strongly associated with a stimulus that the object or event is associated with that state from then on	x		
3. Positive and negative anchors are just as easy to set up *So be careful that you don't set up negative anchors in the classroom that put people off learning*	x		
4. Anchors need to be visual to be really useful *Anchors can be associated with any of the senses. Music can be effectively used in the classroom to elicit certain moods, as could aromas or visual stimuli*		x	
5. Old negative experiences can be collapsed using anchors *Anchors can be collapsed by creating a very powerful positive state stronger than the negative state to collapse the negative anchor*	x		
6. Motivation to get a task done more easily can be overcome by setting anchors *Anchors can be used to get over the inertia of starting a task*	x		
7. You cannot take powerful states that are inside you and move them to any object, time or place *In NLP we use powerful states and project them to other places to enable new things to be achieved*		x	
8. You can get into states and transfer them to others so they can experience it for themselves; you can do this via metaphors, anecdotes or your passion of using skilled language	x		
9. The more you bring up powerful states and place them on objects or yourself (for instance a knuckle, knee or table top), the more these states can build and multiply the strength	x		
10. If you or a pupil is not in a good state, you can access their own internal anchors by asking them what they love in their life. *When you see them inside that state, you can introduce the negative state and it should disappear*		x	

11. Your classroom and home are full of anchors, you can make these even more effective by setting them consciously	x		
12. Any situation or event can be reframed more positively or negatively	x		
13. Presenting your reframe as a metaphor or question will engage the listener better than a bold statement	x		
14. Reframing has to be verbal *You can reframe simply by using body language, sometimes you can do this inadvertently and negatively so you need to be careful to avoid this*		x	
15. The words we use to communicate whether it be through speech, sign or writing are interpretations devised by humans for the purpose of conveying meaning	x		
16. Metaphor is good for both introducing and reviewing sessions	x		
17. Using metaphor well in the classroom is hard to do and requires years of practice *Using metaphor can be started simply and skills gradually developed*		x	
18. You need to have built up excellent rapport with your class before you start using metaphor	x		
19. Metaphor is one of the most powerful tools in a teacher's tool kit	x		

Chapter 5 quiz

	True	False	Maybe
1. Our language is distorted, deleted and generalized by our unconscious (sub-dominant) mind	x		
2. The Meta Model is a collection of vague statements		x	
3. Effective challenging of a person's limiting language needs to be done patiently	x		
4. The Meta Model enables you to identify when a person is using sloppy thinking	x		

5. Awareness of sloppy thinking enables you to reduce misunderstanding and make communication clearer	x		
6. Distortion is the key to creativity	x		
7. A lost performative recovers the choice *Recovers source of the belief, the Performative, strategy for the belief*		x	
8. Complex equivalence means two experiences are interpreted as being synonymous	x		
9. The question 'how specifically?' is great for clarifying sloppy thinking	x		
10. The Milton Model uses vague language to your advantage	x		
11. The Milton Model patterns should never be used to confuse anyone	x		
12. Embedded commands can be used to place important points in the class	x		
13. The Milton Model and Meta Model are two distinct and exclusive systems *The systems work together and complement each other*		x	

Chapter 6 quiz

	True	False	Maybe
1. Goal setting is as much about what you decide not to do as what you decide to do	x		
2. Goals are most attainable when they come from natural motivation	x		
3. Visualising your goal enables you to check if you are congruent with the goal	x		
4. The first question to ask when goal setting is 'how do I know I don't have what I want already?'	x		
5. It is OK to set targets for children in school stating behaviours we don't want them to do *We cannot conceptualise the negative so if you do not want something, describe what it is you do want to see rather than set up an image in the mind of what you don't want to see*		x	

References and further reading

Bandler, R. and Grinder, J. T. (1975) *The Structure of Magic: A Book About Language and Therapy. Volume 1*. Palo Alto, CA: Science and Behavior Books.

Bandler, R. and Grinder, J. T. (1976) *The Structure of Magic. Volume II*. Palo Alto, CA: Science and Behavior Books.

Bandler, R. and Grinder, J. T. (1979) *Frogs into Princes: Neuro Linguistic Programming*. Moab, UT: Real People Press.

Bostic St. Clair, C. and Grinder, J. (2001) *Whispering In The Wind*. Scotts Valley, CA: J & C Enterprises.

Brockman, W. (1980) *Dissertation Abstracts International*

Bruner, J. S. (1996) *The Culture of Education*. Cambridge, MA: Harvard University Press.

Buzan, T. (2003) *Mind Maps for Kids: An Introduction*. London: Thorsons.

Chasse, B., Vicente, M. and Arntz, W. (2006) 'What the Bleep – Down the Rabbit Hole', Revolver Entertainment (DVD).

Chopra, D. (1989) *Quantum Healing – Exploring the Frontiers of Mind/Body Medicine*. New York State: Bantam Books.

Csikszentmihalyi, M. (1991) *Flow: The Psychology of Optimal Experience*. New York: Harper Perennial (Harper & Rowe).

Einspruch, E. L. and Forman, B. D. (1985) 'Observations concerning research literature on Neuro-Linguistic Programming', *Journal of Counseling Psychology*, **32**(4), 589–96.

Elich, M., Thompson, R. W. and Miller, L. (1985) 'Mental imagery as revealed by eye movements and spoken predicates: A test of neurolinguistic programming', *Journal of Counseling Psychology*, **32**(4), 622–5.

Ellickson, J. (1983) 'Representational systems and eye movements in an interview', *Journal of Counseling Psychology*, **30**(3), 339–45.

Falzett, W. (1981) 'Matched versus unmatched primary representational systems and their relationship to perceived trustworthiness in a counseling analog', *Journal of Counseling Psychology*, **28**, 305–308.

Feinburg, S. and Mindess, M. (1994) *Eliciting Children's Full Potential: Designing and Evaluating Developmentally Based Programs for Young Children*. Pacific Grove, CA: Brooks/Cole.

Fraser, D. (2006) 'The creative potential of metaphorical writing in the literacy classroom', *English Teaching: Practice and Critique'*, **5**(2), 93–108.

Gendler, J. (1988) *The Book of Qualities*. New York: Harper & Row.

Grace, P. (1987) *Patricia Grace: Selected Stories*. Auckland: Penguin Books.

Grinder, M. (1991) *Righting the Educational Conveyor Belt*. USA: Metamorphous Press.

Gumm, W., Walker, M. and Day, H. (1982) 'Neurolinguistic programming: Method or myth?', *Journal of Counseling Psychology*, **29**(3), 327–30.

Hammer, A. L. (1983) 'Matching perceptual predicates: Effect on perceived empathy in a counselling analogue', *Journal of Counseling Psychology*, **30**, 2172–9.

Hawkes, T. (1972) *Metaphor: The Critical Idiom*. London: Methuen.

Hill, N. (1937) *Think and Grow Rich*. Meriden, Conn.: The Ralston Society. Also at www.sacred-texts.com

Kessler, R. (2000) *The Soul of Education: Helping Students Find Connection, Compassion, and Character at School*. Alexandria, VA: ASCD.

Koestler, A. (1970) *The Act of Creation*. London: Pan Books.

Korzybski. A. (1931) *Science and Sanity*. Institute of General Semantics.

Lakoff, G. and Johnson, M. (1980) *Metaphors We Live By*. Chicago, IL: Chicago University Press.

Lawly, J. D. and Tompkins, P. L. (2006) *Metaphors in Mind: Transformation Through Symbolic Modelling*. London: Developing Company Press.

McDermott, I. and Jago, W. (2001) *Brief NLP Therapy (Brief Therapies series)*. London: Sage.

Mednick, S. A. (1962) 'The associative basis of the creative process', *Psychological Review*, **69**, 220–7.

Mercer, N. And Littleton, K. (2007) *Dialogue and the Development of Children's Thinking. A Sociocultural Approach*. London: Routledge.

Pert, C. (1999) *Molecules of Emotion: Why You Feel the Way You Feel*. New York: Pocket Books.

Piaget, J. and Inhelder, B. (1969) *The Psychology of the Child*. New York: Basic Books.

Richardson, E. S. (1988) *Children with a Gift in Writing: Book Two*. Henderson, New Zealand: Richardson Printing (E. S. Richardson).

Rosen, S. and M. Erikson (1991) *My Voice Will Go with You: Teaching Tales of Milton H. Erikson* (New edition). New York: W. W. Norton & Co.

Rowe, M. (1986) 'Wait time: slowing down may be a way of speeding up', *Journal of Teacher Education*, **37**, 43–50.

Shapiro, F. (1995) *Eye Movement Desensitization and Reprocessing: Basic Principles, Protocols, and Procedures*. New York: Guilford Press.

Skinner, H. and Stephens, P. (2003) 'Speaking the same language: exploring the relevance of NLP to marketing communications', *Journal of Marketing Communications*, **9**(3), 177–92.

Spohrer, K. (2007) *Teaching NLP in the Classroom*. London: Continuum.

Sternberg, R. J. (ed.) (2004) *The Nature of Creativity*. New York: Cambridge University Press, pp. 43–75.

Talbot, M. (1996) *The Holographic Universe*. New York and London: HarperCollins.

Torrance, E. P. (1999) 'Student teachers' beliefs about creativity', *British Educational Research* Journal, **25**(2), 225–43.

Vygotsky, L. S. (1962) *Thought and Language* (trans. E. Hanfmann and G. Vakar). Cambridge, MA: MIT Press. (Original work published 1934.)

Winner, E. (1997) *The Point of Words: Children's Understanding of Metaphor and Irony*. Cambridge, MA: Harvard University Press.

Appendix

Poems on metaphor reproduced by kind permission of Deborah Fraser, 'The creative potential of metaphorical writing in the literacy classroom', *English Teaching: Practice and Critique*, 2006, **5**(2), 93–108.

Glum

Glum wears grey and black robes and cloaks
And he is 78 years old.
He lives in a dark, dark cave
He hasn't really done anything mainly because he mopes around
And mutters to himself.
He has no friends
And he despises Laughter, Happiness and Humour
Because they take too much pleasure in life.
Glum's bed is made out of thunder clouds
And his pillow is lightning.
His only delight is in other peoples UNHAPPINESS.
Beware of Glum he's on the prowl!

(Andrew D., age 10)

Adventurous

Adventurous wears a black shirt
Covered in all types of badges
From places he has visited
Parts of the world as far apart as Mt Everest
And the Japanese Trench
Or the freezing North Pole
And the steaming equator.
He doesn't have a real home
One settled place with friends and family
He has a friend who sees him frequently
Called Curiosity.
They meet at isolated camp sites
In densely packed rain forests
Or on snowy peaks of mountains.

They share spicy foods
From far-away places
With ingredients untried
And plan their next journey.
Adventurous never hesitates
He always takes a risk.

(Andrew H., age 10)

Glory

Every day she will wait till sunset.
She is the daughter of the rise of the sun.
People believe she forms into the golden hemisphere at dawn
And fades at night.
She's clever and rays fling from her arms.
She's addicted to the fire's warning of night.
She will adore the brightness.

(Kate S., age 7)

Secret

Secret is in a ruby-red car.
He is dressed in a sky blue shirt and pants
But deep inside him his soul is as black
As the opals in a cave
Reflecting away any good.
He prances around like Excited or Handsome
But he observes every detail
And tells his boss Death
Everything he sees.
Death flings him a bag of gold coins
And he scurries off from the underworld
Up to the overworld
Where he prances off again
Ready to do anything
For the gold coins he is carrying.

(Shaun, age 9)

Greed

Greed wears expensive dark trench coats.
I first met Greed when I was two.
Suddenly Greed started to filter through my skin.
While I tried to resist him,
Like a tsunami
Another flourish of Greed came over me
And I started piling lollipops
In the trolley
At the supermarket.
My brief encounter with Greed was not pleasant.
Don't ask him to dinner as he'll only want more and more
And when his stomach starts to ache
He'll blame it all on you.

(Alan, age 10)

Passion

Passion is single minded
She is an obsession
Demanding attention
Yet quiet in contemplation.
She can be a follower
As well as a leader.
Passion is her own style.

(Brie, age 11)

Index

accessing cues 33, 43, 45, 144
action filter 24
ambiguity 112
anchor/anchoring 36, 37, 57–68, 83–85, 132, 134
association 57, 58, 61, 76, 114
auditory 19, 28, 33, 35, 41, 42, 45, 46, 50, 52, 62, 136
auditory digital 35, 46
away from 22, 23, 134

Bandler, Richard 1, 2, 33, 48, 49, 87, 88, 146
belief, limiting 5, 12, 87, 89, 90, 119
Brockman, W 43, 48
Buzan, T. 118

calibrate/calibration 17, 25, 35, 40, 49, 75, 99, 117, 134, 137, 140, 141
cause-effect 91, 100, 105
Chopra, D. 32
chunk/chunking 13, 24, 25, 27, 28, 36, 37, 40, 101, 141, 142
chunk size 24, 28, 141, 142
comparative deletions 96, 101
complex equivalence 94, 100, 105, 122, 145
congruence/congruent 49, 55, 117, 126, 128, 133, 134, 145
conversational postulates 111
context reframe 135
context 12, 16, 37, 38, 42, 45, 49, 70, 71, 82, 83, 88, 97, 110–112, 128, 135, 137, 139
Csikszentmihalyi, M. 21

deep structure 89
deletion 21, 87 -90, 95, 96, 101, 109, 135
dissociation 135
direction filter 22, 40, 140
distortion 21, 87, 88, 89, 90, 100, 102, 122, 135, 145
double bind 110

ecology/ecological 129, 130, 135
Einspruch, E.L 49
Ellickson, J 48

Eye Movement Desensitization and Reprocessing EMDR 37–39, 56, 142
extended quote 111
embedded commands 110, 111, 122, 135, 145
external behaviour filter 25
eye accessing cues 33, 35

filters 6, 12, 17, 19, 21, 22, 24, 25, 40, 87, 88, 125, 126, 129, 134, 140
Frazer, D. 78, 159
future pace 135

Gendler, J. 78
generalization 20, 87–90, 94, 100, 106, 135
goals 124
Grinder, John 1, 2, 33, 48, 49, 87, 88, 146, 147
Grinder, Michael 42
gustatory 41, 42

Inhelder, B 72
intention 13, 69, 71, 87, 113, 135
internal representation 19, 132, 135, 137

Johnson, M 74
journal 1, 14, 39, 68, 74, 84, 101, 114, 121, 132

kinaesthetic 17, 33–35, 41, 42, 45–50, 52, 54, 55, 61, 63, 80, 134, 136, 142
Korzybski, A. 3, 7, 69, 87

Lakoff, G 74
language of persuasion 114
lead system 136
learning styles 1, 41, 42, 47, 61, 75
Littleton, K 116
lost performative 98, 100, 104, 122, 145

matching 27–29, 40, 43, 136, 137, 140, 141, 167
Mercer, N 116

meta 74, 87–91, 93, 95, 97–103, 107, 114,
    121, 122, 136, 144, 145
meta model 87–90, 95, 98, 99–103, 114,
    122, 136, 144, 145
metaphor 2, 3, 31, 68, 69, 73–86, 102, 107,
    136, 137, 143, 144, 147–149
Milton model 87, 101–103, 113, 114, 121,
    122, 136, 145
mind read 17, 90, 92, 100, 103, 104, 112,
    134
mirroring 26–28, 40, 136, 140, 142
modal operators 95, 100, 107
model/modelling/modelled 1, 5, 6, 9, 14, 15,
    19, 33, 43, 48, 73, 87–89, 98, 103, 130,
    136, 138
model of the world 73, 87, 89, 103

nominalization 93, 101, 107, 136
narrative approach 79
non-verbal 73, 136

olfactory 41, 42
outcomes 83, 100, 132, 136

pacing 31, 43, 82, 104, 105, 107, 109,
    136
pace current experience 109
perceptions 5, 136
Pert, C 5
Piaget, J 72
physiology 12, 19, 59, 137
predicate 48, 52, 146, 147
preferred system 48, 136

presupposition 1, 3–15, 30, 69, 71, 73, 90,
    91, 100, 102, 106, 137, 138

rapport 2, 3, 8, 11, 15, 17, 19, 26–32, 43, 49,
    54–56, 70, 73, 86, 89, 99, 101, 104, 107,
    108, 116, 117, 136–138, 140–142, 144
reframing 57, 68, 70, 71–74, 83–85, 135,
    137, 144
referential index 97
representational systems 41–43, 45, 46, 49,
    50, 146
resources 8, 11, 12, 14, 16, 59, 67, 68, 82, 83,
    101, 102, 124, 128, 137, 139
resourceful state 62
Rowe, M 114

sensory acuity 17, 137
Shapiro, F 37
state 18, 19, 57–69, 85, 97, 100–103, 106,
    109, 115, 125, 129, 134, 136, 143, 144
strategy 20, 21, 36, 42, 43, 61, 83, 100, 107,
    116, 119, 145

tag question 108
Talbot, M 125

'What the Bleep' 5

unconscious mind 12, 27, 39, 75, 84, 119,
    131, 136, 137
universals 94
unspecified verbs 96, 101
utilization 113